No Bass, No Party

Gary Shea

Digital ISBNs
EPUB 9780228634522
Kindle 9780228634539
B&N Nook 9780228634546
PDF 9780228634553

Print ISBNs
Amazon print 9780228634560
Ingram Spark 9780228634577
Barnes & Noble 9780228634584
BWL Print 9780228634591

BWL Publishing Inc.

Books we love to write ...
Authors around the world.

http://bwlpublishing.ca

Copyright 2024 by Gary Shea
Editor JD Shipton
Cover artist Michelle Lee
Cover photo by Christopher Collins

All rights reserved. Without limiting the rights under copyright reserved above, no part of this publication may be reproduced, stored in or introduced into a retrieval system, or transmitted, in any form, or by any means (electronic, mechanical, photocopying, recording, or otherwise) without the prior written permission of both the copyright owner and the publisher of this book

Dedication

This book is dedicated to my stepson Peter Goyke who we recently lost to kidney disease. He was a great audience and a masterful storyteller in his own right.

Acknowledgements

Thanks to JD Shipton and the staff at BWL Publishing. I am extremely grateful to Jay BC for inviting me to actually take the time to write my story in my own words. Kudos to my friend and author Jerry Garrish for his insight and encouragement. Eternal gratitude to my wife Caren Kapson for her hard work and direction behind the scenes.

Table of Contents

Chapter 1 7

Chapter 2 10

Chapter 3 16

Chapter 4 21

Chapter 5 29

Chapter 6 71

Chapter 7 75

Chapter 8 78

Chapter 9 83

Chapter 10 87

Chapter 11 90

Gallery 95

Chapter 12 117

Chapter 13 125

Chapter 14..129

Chapter 15..135

Chapter 16..142

Chapter 17..147

Chapter 18 153

Chapter 19..157

Chapter 20 162

Chapter 21.. 171

Chapter 22 175

Chapter 1

It was Christmas time, December 27th 1950. The Feast Of Saint John. General Douglas MacArthur had just landed in Korea   Nat King Cole had the number one hit song with Mona Lisa, and a howling snowstorm was making its way through the Naugatuck Valley in Connecticut. A Waterbury Police patrol car had just received a radio call to proceed to St. Mary's hospital a.s.a.p. The call was special to patrolman Joseph J. Shea as his wife had just given birth to their first child. Suddenly, cut off by another car in the storm, he found his patrol car barreling down a steep hill toward the raging Naugatuck river. He eventually regained control, inches from going over the guard rail and plunging into the night-black freezing water.

At the hospital he was greeted by his wife Pauline and their new son, Gary Michael Shea. A double Capricorn, tipping the scales at 8.5 lbs. My dad's first reaction was "Whoa, look at all that hair!" Bestowed upon me that birthday was a sense of curiosity and wanderlust, there was music in my family blood, and I was ready to travel far and wide.

When I was brought home a few days later we packed up to move. Moving would become natural to me as I was about to attend a multitude of schools and live at a myriad of addresses. This would ultimately be a beneficial skillset to me as I moved around the world seeking a place for myself in the music industry. We lived on what is known as Pine

Hill. The new Federal Interstate System was coming through and Interstate 84 was going right through our house. .We moved to a new place that winter with better heating.

Things were looking up.

* * *

Growing up there was a lot of music in my house. The air was always filled with the sound of records being played rather than the television. My maternal grandfather played piano and my dad had played drums in a large Boy Scout drum corps.

My dad had an extensive collection of 78 rpm records of all of the famous big bands from the 1930s and 40s, like Duke Ellington, the Dorsey Brothers, and Glenn Miller. When the tv was on, we listened to and watched Frank Sinatra, Bobby Darren, Dean Martin, Tony Bennett, and various singers of all genres.

Showing interest in drumming, my dad would show me how to play flams and paradiddles with his 5 S drumsticks, which I still have. I loved the sound they made on the tabletop and how as they sped up, they became a blur.

I would get all the pots, pans, and oatmeal boxes together and tap away on them with the parade drumsticks and brushes.

My grandfather Henry Schuster played piano for Rudee Valley, America's first big musical star of the Roaring 20's.. He was born with arthritis in his hands and was given piano lessons for therapy.

His four brothers played saxophone and clarinet, playing in bands professionally into their 50's.

With over a dozen of my first cousins, his house was a great place at Christmas time. He would play boogie woogie, all the tunes of the day, and play piano tricks for us like

Chico Marx as everyone sang along. All the cousins would take turns banging on the piano.

I was fascinated by the bass notes. They would sustain longer than the higher octaves with a deep resonant tonality. I didn't care for the tinkling of the higher octaves

Curiously, none of my cousins went on to play music.

My brother Peter took up the piano and became very proficient at it. I love hearing him play as he races over the keyboard in sheer enjoyment.

I had yet to find the instrument that I felt comfortable with.

That was all about to change.

Chapter 2

Sputnik sailed across the nighttime sky, The Sharks and The Jets were competing in West Side Story, Elvis was shaking up the censors on television, and suburbia was in full bloom in the late 50s.

By the age of ten, my parents had bought a new house out at the edge of town where Waterbury met Cheshire. The house smelled of new wood and fresh paint. It was a great place to learn how to ride a bike, climb trees, and make forts in the woods. I had fun experimenting with various toy instruments my brother and I had, like bamboo flutes and xylophones, but nothing really struck me as something that I wanted to play. I really wanted to play the drums but my father said that he didn't like the noise, having been an anti-aircraft gunner in the U.S. Navy during World War Two.

My mom had a friend named Bert, short for Roberta. She lived nearby at the end of Rockaway Avenue with her husband Pete and their two daughters in an old, funky house. The girls were the same age as my brother and I, and we used to play together. Pete was a very nice, balding Italian man with a mustache. Among all the clutter in their house were two old, well traveled guitar cases.

One day Pete took them out and showed us what was inside the cases. I had never seen a real guitar other than what I had seen on TV. He had two early 1950s single cutaway, archtop, jazz guitars. He played a very jazzy guitar style reminiscent of Django Reinhardt. I liked how the guitar resonated within the wooden body and likened it to the strings on the piano. They looked really cool to me. I had never seen a real electric guitar before, especially one that could plug into an amplifier. They seemed very mysterious, also. I sat and listened, watching his fingers form all the jazz chords that he knew how to play. It seemed very complicated and difficult. He let me hold them in my lap and strum the strings. It was all very intriguing, being able to adjust the volume and tone of the guitar with knobs and switches. The guitars had an aura of rebellion to them as everyone kept saying not to touch them, and to be careful. The restrictions made me want to hold the guitar even more out of pure youthful defiance.

At this point we moved again and said goodbye to our neighbors and the mysterious guitars. They had made a lasting impression on me, and I hoped to see more. We were moving down the mountain to Southington.

* * *

It was the era of the transistor radio! Great sounds through a tiny speaker and single earpiece.

Everybody had one. I was listening to all the pop stars of the day in junior high, from Gene Pitney, Elvis, Jan and Dean, The Ronettes, Bobby Rydell, The Four Seasons, The Beach Boys, The Ventures, and of course all of the Motown groups.

During that period of my life I was car crazy and had become very good at making model cars. I had about 40 all around my bedroom and had won a few awards at the local hardware store and the state fairs. I carved a AA fuel dragster out of a block of balsa wood. I used all my best parts and sprayed it with a dozen coats of red candy apple paint. That was the height of my collection at that point.

At night. I would listen to my radio under the covers and pick up stations far away in Chicago, St Louis, W. Virginia, and New York City and for the first time really started listening to music. What was the difference between the different singers? Why did I like certain songs but not others? I didn't realize it was the bass lines of all those songs that I was grooving along to while tapping my foot in time with the beat.

My backyard was the town's municipal parking lot. We lived over a tavern next to the dry cleaners, the Italian grocery store, the barber shop, the furniture store, etc.

On the next corner was The Popular Restaurant, which had the best food and pizza in town. They had a banquet room where many wedding receptions were held. We would sit outside the back doors on our bicycles and watch the bands carry their gear inside. One of the more popular bands in town were the Merrays. Their bass player, Butch Hart, would become a good friend of mine.

The band looked great in their shark-skin suits, pointy shoes, and Elvis haircuts. They were four or five years older with driver's licenses and my friends and I looked up to those guys. We would hang out by the back doors and listen to them play, and I began thinking that playing music might be pretty cool.

One day my brother came home upset that while riding his bike, three brothers had given him a hard time. I took off on my bike ready to defend my brother. Of the three, Larry was my brother's age and Billy and Mark were younger. They apologized saying they didn't mean it and the five of us became friends.

When I went to their house eventually, two things surprised me. They had three younger sisters and Larry had a full set of Kent red sparkle drums. He looked like a shorter version of James Dean and was an excellent drummer. As I continued to go visit him I met his friend, Norby. He had a cheap Kay electric guitar and when something would go wrong with it he would throw it across the room. Norby didn't pursue music but became the owner of a successful custom automotive paint shop, and I would play in a band with Larry in two years time.

I listened to the two of them playing along to Ventures albums, trying to learn songs like Perfidia and Walk Don't Run. Then they moved on to British bands like The Yardbirds and The Animals.

At this point, I decided that I too would get a guitar and delve into this new world of performing music. I was intrigued by what could be done the more you learned how to play. The idea of creating your own songs seemed like a challenge I wanted to take on. First I would have to convince my parents. It was easier said than done.

* * *

What do you do when you ask your father for something major and he says no, no way, forget about it and don't ever ask me again? Well, I know what I did. I went straight to my mother and I worked on her.

I had decided that I wanted an electric guitar. After watching my friends have a great time playing music, I became one of the thousands who went out and bought a guitar during the British Invasion of the late 60s. I loved the Kinks Greatest Hits album with the Gibson Flying V on the cover and the rebellious group photos of The Rolling Stones and The Yardbirds.

My mom was an angel. She was one of six kids who grew up listening to her father's dance bands practice in their living room over the years. She had a dream of going to art school but had to stay home to take care of her younger brother when her mother became very ill. She taught my brother and I how to draw, how to paint, how to sew with a needle and thread, and other dexterous talents. I told her of my desire to get a guitar and we struck a deal together.

We agreed that I could get a guitar with the money I'd saved up if I took a music course and proved to her that I was serious and not just going to waste my money on something frivolous. I swore up and down that I was really serious.

Not far away was a small music store that taught lessons. The owner, Bob Marcucci, was an accordion player by profession but could teach brass instruments and guitar. I signed up for a ten week guitar class in which he would show me the fundamentals of the guitar and loan me a cheap Stella acoustic guitar to practice on. I walked down the street proudly carrying my new guitar friend, regardless if it was inexpensive. "Hey look, I'm playing the guitar!"

I was really geeked and sat in front of him with the guitar, and then he dropped The Bomb. He said, "Do you realize that you are left-handed and you're holding the guitar upside down?" I said, "I know, Paul McCartney plays guitar and bass left-handed." "Yes, that is true" He agreed, "But since you don't know how to play either way, it would be a great benefit for you to learn right handed. No need to buy custom left-handed guitar. They're hard to find and more expensive, so if you could learn how to play the guitar right-handed you would really be doing yourself a favor." Of course, I thought he was crazy at first, but I gave it some thought and realized he was making some kind of sense. So I took his advice and learned how to play right-handed. To this day, I thank him profusely. Being a bass player and being left-handed, I have more strength in my left hand to hold down the bass strings, which I think is a good advantage. Now, playing left handed is beyond awkward.

My dad warmed up to the idea that I was serious about playing the guitar. At the end of the 10 week course he and my mom came in to hear me play. Bob offered them a chance to buy a guitar from him, which was a red, no name, Italian electric with 4 pickups and many rocker switches. I knew from reading the guitar catalogs that what I really wanted was a Fender guitar. In fact, a Fender Stratocaster.

To get started, we went to a Caldor department store and I bought a Japanese Teisco Del Ray electric guitar for $68, and a Silvertone amplifier from Sears with a 12 inch speaker. I used my life savings from shoveling snow for the neighborhood store owners on my street and picking apples for two seasons at Lewis Farms

I was off and running among the ranks of the many new guitar players in my town.

Chapter 3

I was a big fan of The Beach Boys. Through the car-oriented songs, I could imagine the smell of the tires burning up the asphalt and screaming down the street. The first record I ever bought was their Little Deuce Coupe album. One of the songs on the record was called 409. The lyric was." Well I saved my money and I saved my dimes before I knew there would be a time when I would buy a brand new 409. Well, I didn't buy a brand new Chevrolet car with a 409 cubic inch engine, but I was about to buy my new guitar. Slim Boucher had a cousin named Rainy Rivers (Rene Riviere) who was a well-known country and western guitarist. He owned a music store called River's Guitar Center in New Britain, Connecticut. New Britain was nicknamed New Brinski due to its large Polish population. I had been there before and knew they had what I wanted. It was home to world-famous Stanley Tools, and Rivers' music store was the largest music store I'd ever seen. It was very well stocked with all the famous brands of guitars, drums, and keyboards.

When the great day came, my mother drove my brother, Peter, my friend Jerry, and me to the store. I had a bank envelope with my hard-earned three hundred dollars. I gave up $265.00 for a beautiful brand-new, 1965 Fender Stratocaster guitar in a sunburst finish with a white pick guard. The guitar was gorgeous, with a contoured body that fit against my side perfectly. It also came with a plush-lined hard shell case. Everything was tuned properly and the guitar played like butter. It was so much easier to play than the inexpensive Japanese guitar I was leaving behind. I don't think I slept once that night. I kept getting up and looking to make sure it was still there next to my bedside. Sometimes I would just open the case and smell the fragrance of rosewood, chrome, and furniture polish. A dream came true. Little did I know that this was just a steppingstone to something far greater than I had ever imagined.

*　*　*

In those days there was no such thing as the internet or social media. There was no YouTube. The only tubes I knew of were the inner tubes we used when we went swimming at the lake, and tubes of Brylcreem, which I used to grease my hair back like Elvis Presley. As the jingle went, "　Brylcreem: a little dab'll do you, Brylcreem: you'll look so debonair". I used 2 dabs just to make sure. There were no online tutorials or free videos available for me to expand my musical knowledge like there are today. Writing tablature had not come into vogue. You either learned how to read sheet music, or you played by ear if you could. I had the first three or four How To Play The Guitar instruction books by the great Mel Bay. It was time to expand my musical lessons, and living in small town there weren't many options. I heard about a teacher named Slim Boucher who happened to be an excellent jazz guitarist. He began to teach me jazz arrangements of songs like Roger Miller's "King Of The Road". He told me if I could learn this style when I turned 18, I could play in the Catskills at Lake George and make good money. My guitar playing was improving. The only drawback was that Slim had a beautiful daughter that was a couple of years older. Every time she walked into the room, the room went silent and I went into a trance. I heard nothing of what he was talking about until she left. I knew that the music theory that Slim was teaching me was very important and would be the key to improving my guitar playing. On the other hand, I was anxious to learn more of the rock songs of the great bands I was listening to. I said thanks and moved on. My friends told me about a younger guitarist from my high school, saying he was the best lead guitarist in town. His name was Jerry Talbot. Little did we know that ten years later I would be playing to thousands at Madison Square Garden and he would be my guitar tech. Jerry loved high school so much that he stayed an extra two years he was a junior and going on nineteen. As the class comedian he was always in trouble and I was often enough guilty by association. He *was* the best guitarist at the time, however, and began to show me how to play 12 bar blues and songs by The Stones, The Beatles, and The Rascals. He would come over to my house and show me how this goes here and that goes there. I would watch his fingers and copy what he was doing. He had a real cool top-of-the-line Sears and Roebuck electric guitar in red sunburst.

In school I would hide a chord chart book for guitar inside my textbook. I would stare at all the domino-looking chord formations and memorize them. Once in a while I would be called upon by the teacher to answer a question, not having the faintest clue where we were, but damn, I knew what an E flat major seventh chord looked like.

* * *

It was now time to get out and play music with other people. Time to make some noise. There is joy and satisfaction to be had playing music within a tight group and being in front of a hungry crowd. Nothing beats playing live music with a real drummer and other musicians, where you can feel what they're doing and anticipate what happens next. My friend Jerry said we should go over to his friend Billy Hayes' and jam together, as Billy was one of the best drummers around. He had a nice set of Rogers drums in a black pearl finish down in his family's basement. Curiously, Billy had stage fright and would not play in public. His family supported us coming over on weekends and making noise though, and it was a wonderful place to go and hang out, especially during the long winters. Mr. and Mrs. Hayes were terrific. Billy, nicknamed "Crowbar", had an amazing record collection. I got to listen in depth to everyone from Bob Dylan to Wilson Pickett. We heard Buddy Guy and The Paul Butterfield Blues Band, as well as all of the new English bands that were coming up. Sam and Dave, The Young Rascals, and Mose Allison were all on the ever-revolving turntable. As well as Jerry and myself, our friend Val Mongillo played with us. His guitar was a beautiful red Guild Starfire. He was studying classical violin and would one day join the Vermont Symphony. Jerry's older brother, Mike, would come down once in a while. He was in the Army in Germany and had the biggest amplifier we'd ever seen. It was a Sears Silvertone amp with 6, 10 inch speakers. It was so big. It had wheels and we sometimes just sat around it and marveled at how cool it was. Amid the sound of all these guitars and drums I felt there was something missing. I couldn't quite place what I wasn't hearing, but it was about to hit me like a ton of bricks and change my life forever.

 Did you ever come across something you just had to have? Something you couldn't put down or walk away from? An item that just felt so right?

 One afternoon after high school Jerry and I drove to Carl's Electronics in Meriden, Connecticut. Carl's was an independently owned electronics and TV appliance repair store. Carl had a large stand-alone tube tester, which we were going to use to test the tubes of our amplifiers. Hanging on the walls above all the radios and TVs, were a dozen used electric guitars for sale. I looked around the room and found myself drawn to a 1964 Fender Precision bass. I had recently purchased a brand new 1965 Fender Stratocaster.

I stared at it and couldn't believe how big it was. I took it off the wall and said to Jerry, "Man this is like an aircraft carrier, it's so large." It felt enormous compared to an electric guitar and I couldn't get over how big the strings were. It had all the Fender features: contour body, tortoise pick guard, and sunburst paint job. Huge tuning pegs on a very long rosewood neck connected toa massive bridge covered by a large chrome bell. Being a tall kid, it felt great in my hands and very comfortable.

When we plugged it into an amplifier, everything in the store started to rattle and rumble. I had never felt that kind of low power from an electric guitar'

I asked how much it was and Carl said $125.00 with the Fender case. The electric bass seemed magical to me and even though I had just bought the guitar of my dreams, I felt it beckoning. "Try me, you'll like it, you'll never go back," She whispered.

Jerry laughed and said "'What are you going to do with that?" I said, "Hell, I'm going to buy it!" I had some extra money saved up and said "sold." I told Carl "I'll take it, wrap it up, I'm taking it home." It was the missing sound I was looking for. The bass thumped like a heartbeat and pumped the groove of the music from there on after.

That's the day I became a bass player, vowing to shake the world, and I've never looked back.

Chapter 4

In a mad moment of musical inspiration, I had turned myself upside down. Rather than being one of the many guitar players around, I was about to be the guy who drove the train. The guy on bass who set the groove that everyone danced to. Along with the drums, I would set the foundation of all the music that we played. The bass is the connection between the beat and the rhythm. I really could shake the floor and the walls with this thing, and that really appealed to me.

My used bass was a cousin of my brand new guitar. They were both made in the same factory in Fullerton California by a genius named Leo Fender. The man wasn't a musician but was amazing with electronics and woodworking. He single handedly invented some iconic instruments that have stood the test of time. 95% of songs that were recorded from the 1950's and 60's, were made on a Fender bass. The Beatles were the exception, with Paul McCartney playing the German Hofner bass shaped like a violin.

The bass was larger but had the same design of the beautifully contoured body of my Stratocaster. It felt great in my hands. It couldn't have been designed any simpler. There were two control knobs, one for volume and one for tone. The tone rolled between bass and treble. It also came with a plush lined hard case, and judging by some of the dings, it had seen some action. It immediately felt like an old friend.

What I discovered was that there weren't many bass players around. Because of that I could always find gigs for myself. The trick now was to teach myself how to play it, since there weren't many others to learn from in my area.

I brought my new bass to Billy Hayes' house and began the task of learning the bass lines of the songs we've been playing. I think the first song I learned on the bass was If I needed Someone by The Beatles. Another was Gimme Some Lovin by The Spencer Davis group. I learned how to play with the drummer and become a unit. The kick drum and where I placed my notes, created a driving force. I taught myself walking bass and studied how the left hand of the piano and the bass had a lot in common, determining what I played on the bass.

I paid $125.00 for my used 1965 Fender Precision Bass. Very similar to the bass used by the great James Jamerson on all of the Motown recordings.

Those vintage basses today sell for over $10,000.00 and up. Who knew back then??

* * *

Knock knock knock, BAM BAM BAM! What do you do when opportunity starts hammering at your door like a cop at 2am for a noise complaint? Do you stand back and say "gee, I'm not sure, what if things go wrong and things don't work out?" Or do you stand up at the plate and take a wild swing, hoping for a home run? Me, I'm all about going for it. Stand at the plate and give it your best shot. As the saying goes, he who hesitates loses. It was a trait that would serve me well over the years. Knock knock bam bam: It was Jerry Talbot beating on our back door. We lived on the 2nd floor and our back door had no doorbell. You had to knock loudly. Jerry was standing out in the freezing cold and snow yelling, let me in!

It was the week before Christmas and there was lots of action in the kitchen with baking and preparation. Jerry came in, said hello to my mom and asked if we could talk in my room. I said sure as he entered and I closed the door. He said he had great news. A guitarist friend of his whom he had met going to Wilcox Tech in Meriden Ct. had a friend that played organ. They were all a few years older than me and had some experience playing in other bands. They were both from neighboring Plainville and knew a good drummer from Bristol. There was a plan to start a band together. The big question was, would I like to be the bass player? Of course I said, "Hell yeah", and we began laying out a game plan.

My 16th birthday was a few days before and it was looking good.

We decided to meet at guitarist Bill Tomlin's parents' house on New Year's Day 1967. Peter Brown the organist, and drummer Bill Buckland would meet us there. A friend gave Jerry and myself a ride over with our guitars and amps. Bill Tomlin's parents were away for the day and we set up our gear in their rec room.

We had four or five songs that we mutually knew together and blasted away. It was a great addition to have someone playing keyboards. It gave the band a much wider musical landscape and allowed us to play songs like Light My Fire and Come On Up.

As evening drew near, we had to end the fun before Bill's parents got back and heard the racket we were making in their beautiful home. Our rehearsal had gone well and we mutually decided to do it again soon. There was a bigger problem. Jerry and I had no ride back to Southington. We scratched our heads then Bill said, "I know what we'll do". Bill's father was a detective for the Connecticut State Police and sitting in the driveway was a brand new Connecticut State Police unmarked Ford sedan, with the keys hanging from a hook by the kitchen back door. Bill grinned, "Let's Do It!"

We loaded our gear in the State Police car as quickly as we could not to arouse suspicion from the neighbors. The car was outfitted with dual spotlights, police radio, and an array of lights on the both dashboards. We headed out onto the city streets glad that it was dark due to daylight saving time. Bill took the backroads but there at an intersection was a Plainville Police car coming straight at us. Jerry and I scrunched down saying our prayers. Bill waved at the cop as we passed by. He waved back and kept going. We yelled and screamed at our good fortune.

Bill got both of us home safely and managed to get home before his Dad did without ever getting caught. What a way to start the New Year off. I really liked the mischief we got ourselves into and decided that evening that I wanted to pursue the band thing further. I was in!

* * *

It was almost unanimous: No way! Not here you're not! Forget it! and Take that noise somewhere else! Sounded like the names of racehorses. Four out of five sets of parents said no to us rehearsing at their homes for various reasons. Since our friend Bill Hayes didn't want to be in the band due to his stage fright, that left his house out as a place we could practice. We needed a place where we could leave our gear set up and somewhere we could play more than one or two days a week.

As I said earlier, my Mom was one of six kids who grew up with their piano playing father rehearsing in their front room, horn section and all. My Dad had taken a second shift job at the junior high school from 3pm to 11pm weekdays. Since he wouldn't be around to hear our commotion, they gave us the green light. Mom said we could use the attic weeknights from 7pm to 9 pm.

My house at 21 Liberty Street became the band's new home base for the next year and a half. There were no Better Homes and Gardens around there. There were run-down apartments across the street fueled by cheap wine and beer. My neighbors were living primarily on food stamps and welfare. Ideal Drop Forge was a block away in our industrial neighborhood. The forge shook the house, and I would use the steady banging as a metronome.

The tavern that we lived over had closed down to be made into two apartments eventually. Our rental apartment had three bedrooms with front and backdoor staircases. Above that was a half-finished attic the length of the house with a wooden floor and peaked roof. You could stand upright in most of it. The attic was cold as hell in the winter and hot as hell in the summer. My Mom could flick the power from my bedroom light switch which was the signal to cool it down up there when our tv began skipping, or when my brother would be trying to do his homework. As we began playing gigs, all the gear went up the front staircase late at night, through my bedroom and up the attic stairs that you couldn't stand up straight on.

As well as the five of us, there were always three or four friends hanging around. Jerry and I worked after school until 6pm, and my Mom would feed everyone, usually spaghetti. She liked our new big family and everyone loved her. She became known as "Ma Shea" to the troops and was our great defender from the neighbors.

Her nurturing and charity got us through those high school years where we could move on to rehearsing in warehouses and studios. She always maintained to friends and relatives that for all of our noise and shenanigans, she always knew where we were. She was the rock in our progress and the woman behind our success.

***

We were like the eruption of a new volcano in the middle of that 1967 winter. Our recent partnership was red hot and very active. Everyone got along well and The Attic became our new headquarters and clubhouse. It was where all strategic planning was conducted as we rehearsed over and over again in the quest for musical perfection.

The camaraderie was all new to me up to this point. In my life I had usually just one close friend here and there over the years. Now I was part of a new family, a cool group of guys that wanted to make a mark in music. We dreamed of us being on the radio and playing alongside famous bands. All of a sudden, I was part of a teenage network that was spread among three high schools in three different towns. Our circle of 5 guys turned into an association of 50. I had many new friends and lots of support. The Attic became a popular place.

Bill Tomlin brought up the subject of getting a manager. We had yet to play anywhere but we wanted to be professional. We decided a manager would be a good asset. There was the son of a very successful local businessman named Gary Przbilski that Bill wanted us to meet. He was a few years older and had put on some dances locally. He seemed to know his way around the music business as far as we could tell.

The first order of business was what to name the band?

We had been thinking of calling ourselves The Wrong Bunch. Gary came up with the idea of a band called The Insane.

He had an idea of us appearing on stage in straightjackets. He would take a starter gun and shoot each one of us to begin playing. We thought that was a little over the top. Then along came Alice Cooper so maybe he had a good idea? We liked The Insane because it sounded rebellious.

We had our first gig booked coming up on January 21st at The Plainville Knights Of Columbus. We had rehearsed almost every night since our first time together at Bill Tomlin's house and put together a set of songs for maximum impact. Our best volley would be Substitute and My Generation by The Who. Being strong, dynamic and relentless was our goal. Having observed all of the bands in the area we knew how we wanted to present ourselves and what the competition was. Our first time out was to play in a Battle of The Bands up against three other groups. Bill Tomlin and Peter Brown our keyboard player, were both from Plainville, with drummer Bill Buckland from neighboring Bristol, and Jerry Talbot and myself, from Southington. We put the word out among our three high schools that we would be playing, trying to recruit as many fans as possible. There would be a combination of judges and crowd response. It was very exciting to pack up our gear and drive off out of town to play live in front of an audience of our peers. We had our top-notch equipment loaded into the half dozen cars of our entourage. The adrenaline began to take effect as we moved out across town to the battlefield, gearing up to competition mode. All of us being focused was our main goal, knowing that was the key to coming across as a professional group rather than a band thrown together just to have a party. Being wintertime, the hall was packed because there were not many places for kids to hang out. Our getting the word out produced a full house of about two hundred people and there was plenty of excitement in the room. With everyone dancing, the temperature inside was at summertime levels: hot and sweaty, unlike our rehearsals in my cold frozen attic rehearsal space. Perfect conditions for a great set. I always liken the first song of the set as being a similar experience to a bull rider in the rodeo coming out of the chute, wide-open and pumped up in the moment. Thrilled, apprehensive, and hanging on, capturing the audience's full attention and you feel like you're being shot out of a cannon. Total excitement from the band's point of view. I put everything I had into my two-note bass intro starting off the set. When the band kicked in behind me I was sent into a dream state similar to when you are underwater and the voices you hear are muffled murmurs. I could hear and feel the rumble of my bass amplifier beneath my feet on the wooden stage, far surpassing the feeling I had the first time I tried out my bass the day I bought it. With the confidence of being well rehearsed, now was the time to shift into the showmanship of moving around and putting on a show. Smile, look people in the eye, and enjoy the ride. As our set progressed, I felt we were doing a pretty good job considering that we had just begun playing together. My suspicions were confirmed as the crowd cheered and the judges announced we were the winners of the one hundred dollars prize money and an 18-inch-tall trophy! The first time out in 21 days and we nailed it. We hugged each other and felt a great sense of accomplishment. The trophy made it around to all the parents' homes like The Stanley Cup with pride and conviction.

    The Insane were up and running and my bass playing career was off with a bang. I was awestruck that I could get paid for doing something that I loved with all my heart and soul. From that day on I never looked back as I set out to follow my dream of being in a world renowned band. I had rehearsed over and over to win the top spot at The Knights of Columbus and now it was time to set my sights on playing at Madison Square Garden in New York City and beyond.

Chapter 5

There's no business like show business like no business I know. So let's get on with the show. Irving Berlin 1946.

With the success of The Insane's first gig I was ready to join the circus and see the world. Looking back over my 50 years of playing music, I got a great inside glimpse of what the music business entailed. I was about to enter a world of ups and downs, and some amazing times I'll always cherish.

I've always maintained that the music business is 85% business and 15% music. Show business is a world of management contracts, record contracts, publishing contracts, and performing contracts to name a few; all written by some lawyers and translated by your own lawyers. Even though I had read some horror stories of other artists' careers and business missteps, I would still one day be personally sued for $1,000,000.00 in a New York City Federal Court. More about that later.

What music instruction books fail to tell you is about the dog-eat-dog world of music publishing. New bands are coerced into signing away the rights of the ownership to their songs in a never-ending battle. Artists are told by managers and record companies that it is all fair for everyone so that they can make their investments back. A manager can charge 20% to the artist and that is 20% of the gross money the artist earns. The artist gets the net income and doesn't see profit until all of the bills and expenditures of doing business are paid, often landing them in the red. A case in point is the band Kansas who assigned

100% of their music publishing rights to Don Kirshner. He made millions with the amount of records they sold. The band saw none of that profit and only made money from playing live.

As I began my musical journey, I was aware of certain situations. Some of these pitfalls were ten to twenty years in my future. Sometimes you have to gamble the ranch hoping nothing goes wrong and that it will pay off for you at the end of the deal. Making it in the music business is like running through a minefield: you can be prepared, but there is also a dash of pure luck involved. Also in the pre internet days you had to be in the right place at the right time.

Let's return to the story of The Insane, where all of these situations had their beginning. They would soon manifest themselves as time moved along in some unsuspected and inevitable ways.

Do you have a memory of a time of year or a season that you hold in a special place in your heart? A time that was magical to you that can never be repeated? Mine would be the winter of 1967. Halfway through my Junior year of high school, The Insane became a band and a brotherhood. Our one desire was to become a good band and rise up the ranks of the music world, emulating our heroes.

Early 1967 was a time when The Beatles had yet to release Sargent Pepper and Jimi Hendrix and Led Zeppelin were still unknown. Whiter Shade of Pale by Procol Harum was not out yet, nor Days of Future passed by The Moody Blues. They would all come along later, in 1967. We listened to the Rascals, Vanilla Fudge, The Paul Butterfield Blues Band, Motown and of course The Stones and The Kinks. The Yardbirds were one of my favorites, but The Who were my all time favorite. They invented heavy music and customized prototype Marshall amplifiers and round wound bass strings. I wanted to sound like John Entwistle and shake the place.

This music was the reason for us to want to form a band. Jerry Talbot and I couldn't wait until school and our jobs at the grocery stores after school were over, so that we could rehearse at my house. We learned songs from my record player and went from dimes to quarters taped to the needle arm as the scratches on the vinyl got deeper and deeper.

Our setlist went from Mustang Sally by Wilson Pickett, to Born In Chicago by Paul Butterfield, to Ferry Across The Mersey by Jerry and Pacemakers, to Slow Down by the Rascals to Substitute, and I can't Explain by The Who. We played a B side song by The Byrds called Why. We thought it was funny because it was the same chord changes as Martha Reeves' song Heatwave. We managed to keep ourselves busy just about every weekend for the next year and a half up to my high school graduation.

The lineup was Jerry Talbot, lead guitar lead vocalist, Billy Tomlin, rhythm guitar, Peter Brown, organ, Bill Buckland, drums, and myself on bass. In the time prior to YouTube tutorials and tablature, Peter acted as our music director in disputes as to what was the correct chord or harmony part in all arguments. Everyone sang background vocals.

We were fortunate to be at the vanguard of the coming onslaught of amazing new rock bands. There was a tremendous amount of new music to enjoy listening to and the bar of musicianship kept getting higher. It made the whole scene blossom with new sounds and merging styles. I was inspired to learn as much as I could and hopefully become part of it.

And so in early 1967 the journey began of The Insane auditioning for clubs, playing Battles Of The Bands, and getting bookings on the circuit in the Southern New England area. We were very successful in getting return engagements. By summertime we were playing at the beach at the George in Misquamicut, Rhode Island and the George in Newington, Connecticut. We played at TV show host Brad Davis's Flingo East and Flingo West. Both clubs had state-of-the-art lighting systems. The band played many times in the Danbury Elks Hall and upstate New York at the Brewster Lanes. We played The Hullabaloo Club in Waterbury and Thetford Academy in Vermont.

The Insane had very good musical equipment. I had a new Fender Bassman amplifier in black Tolex, along with Jerry's Fender Bandmaster and Bill's Dual Showman. Jerry played my Fender Stratocaster while Bill chose a Moserite guitar. My Fender Precision Bass was the same model that James Jameson played on all the Motown hits. Pete Brown had a Farfisa organ and Bill Buckland had Ludwig drums. What we didn't have was our own PA system.

Our new manager Gary Prez, who was 21, proposed we take out a loan for a thousand dollars. With that, we could buy a brand new Kustom 200 watt PA with 2 4x12 / speaker columns in pleated white naugahyde. We would make 10 payments of $100.00 a month and pay off the loan. Rick Derringer and The McCoy's came to Connecticut and we rented our new PA to them for a concert, which took care of the first few bank payments.

I had just turned 16 and talked my dad into getting a van that he and I could share. It was a used 1964 Chevy Corvair Van with no side windows and a bench seat up front. We could get all of our gear and half a dozen of us in it. We usually traveled with an extra 2 or 3 cars of friends, as fights were a common event in the early days of long hair, jealous boyfriends, and different clothes.

On a serious note, we once played The Newington Home For Crippled Children. The hospital had a full-size ballroom, and they wheeled in about 200 kids on beds with all kinds of physical defects. All the kids were elementary school age and they were wonderful. After we played, we walked among them and talked. They thought we were The Beatles. All the kids laughed and teased each other playfully. I signed my first autograph that day and I swore to myself from that day on that I had no real problems. I would be forever thankful for my good fortune, and I've never forgotten the love those kids showed us.

Another first was coming up; We were about to make a record of our original music.

As our first few months progressed rapidly, so too did we. A deal to record a 45 rpm record of two of our songs was being offered to us. That really appealed to us as we always wanted to work on original music and not just be a Top 40 band. With an investment of $500.00, we could record a 45 and have 500 copies pressed. Selling them for two dollars apiece would pay for the recording cost and give us a profit of $500.00. We are about to learn the art of self-promotion and publicity.

On May first, my Mom's birthday, we drove to Plymouth, Connecticut to record on the Allen recording label. We rehearsed our original material well and did a few run-throughs of our songs, "Someone Like You" and "I Can't Prove It". We recorded the music live and the main vocals and background vocals were done after that. All in all we were done in under four hours that day. Everything went as planned and we were really happy with the outcome. Both songs were written by Pete Brown, who also sang the lead vocals. I was happy to do the bass lead-in on the first song "I Can't Prove It". There was also a backup song called "Out On A Limb" that Jerry Talbot had written. When we got our 500 copies, we realized that 100 copies each was a lot to sell after we had all hit up our friends and relatives. We had hundreds of black vinyl records with yellow labels everywhere around the room. We were anxious to try and get one of the songs added to the playlist on the local radio stations. That is easier said than done, as there are only 40 records in the Top 40 and the competition is tough. Both songs by The Insane can be heard on You tube these days, and with much less trouble.

We managed to recoup our initial investment and make a profit of a few hundred dollars. We were in the early days of setting up a merchandise table, just as it is done today. Our friends would hang posters and set up a table at our gigs and help sell our records. The record provided us with another tool in working with booking agents and promoters. The best advantage of our new endeavor was that now we could be billed as Recording Artists.

There are two ways to see a horror show: You can go to the movies or join a band. If things can go wrong, they certainly will. I'm not a pessimist– if I was, I wouldn't have gone as far as I have in music. A manager once told me "There are no problems, only opportunities." Funny how he became a major problem years later.

As an artist or group climbs the ladder of success in the music business, others are needed to help with business and creative ventures. All the managers, lawyers, accountants, and producers that you hire must be trustworthy. They can speak on your behalf and sometimes cut deals unknown to you. Take managers, for example: If they are the ones collecting the money earned it's easy to take your eye off the ball financially. Sometimes it's too late by the time you realize something has gone awry. There are some managers who don't have your best interests at heart. Billy Joel is a good example of this– His brother-in-law was his accountant and nearly bankrupted him by embezzlement.

Another classic story is Rocky and Shirley Davis of Rocshire Records who embezzled $24,000,000.00 from Howard Hughes. Alcatrazz, which had recorded its first album "No Parole" on the Rocshire label, was lucky to have signed a new record deal with Capitol

Records and got out of there a month before The F.B.I. moved in and shut them down. More about this later.

The Insane had gone a long way in a few short months and took the recommendation of guitarist Bill Tomlin to have his friend, Gary Przbilski, a.k.a. Gary Prez, become the manager of the band. There were no contracts other than just a handshake in good faith. Gary Prez was a tall, lanky, long-haired, local guy. He knew a few club owners and was eager to help promote the band. Since he was 21 years old, he was the one who signed for the $1000.00 bank loan to purchase our Kustom PA system. He drove a blue 1965 Plymouth Satellite that had been modified for racing, and he was responsible for naming the group The Insane.

The band held meetings regularly and guitarist Jerry Talbot was very good at writing down what was discussed. He kept a record of what money the band was holding and a description of various deductions. A few pages of those discussions still exist. With the money that the band earned, we would go down to Manny's Music on W. 48th Street in New York City and buy more gear. We had great times down there staring at all of the 8x10 band press photos all over the walls, hoping that one day we too would have our photo up there. We dreamed about playing at Madison Square Garden. We walked the streets of Greenwich Village and bought clothes from England that we couldn't wear to school.

By May of 1967, the music scene was gearing up for the Summer Of Love. Along with it came a series of influential albums. The Beatles would release Sargent Pepper and Jimi Hendrix would come down from Mars and freak out the world with Are You Experienced. It was a revolution in music and culture. In our little part of the Earth in Southern New England we too had a new record to promote. We now had a new addition to our set. It was exciting to be able to play original music for the first time, which elevated us from amateur status to a more professional level. We decided what we needed next was a booking agency. Rather than trying to get gigs on our own, we wanted expert help and we approached Christopher Productions in Hartford, Connecticut.

Our friends, The Blue Beats released their single "Extra Girl" in 1967 on Columbia Records. They opened for Cream's first tour nearby at the Oakdale Theater in Wallingford, Connecticut. The show was booked by Christopher Productions which was headed up by Ken Griffin, the premier DJ in Connecticut for station WPOP 1410 AM. He also managed The Blue Beats. WPOP is credited with helping to break the Four Seasons to national fame. Ken knew everybody in the Connecticut music scene. An audition was arranged in July, 1967 for us to play for Christopher Productions.

Hartford had a river boat named The Dolly Madison that went down the Connecticut River three times per day. We would play for Ken on a Friday night boat ride and play 2 sets. Unknown to us was the fact that the floors of the ship were sheet metal and our amps and microphones were not grounded. We were shocked many times and somehow we got through the evening with nothing serious happening. It didn't make for a relaxed performance. Ken really liked the band and took us under his wing. We started getting better gigs and better money.

We would be booked just about every weekend for the next year. The band was booked that summer at The George and Misquamicut Beach Rhode Island. The George was a very happening place to play. We didn't want to pay for a hotel and wound up in the Waverly, Rhode Island Police station for unlawfully sleeping on the beach. Another gig the following winter had us in Colchester, Connecticut, the home at the time of The Connecticut Dragway. Today the track is owned by Consumer Reports as their test track.

We played during a snowstorm way out in the woods. Out of four bands scheduled to play that night we were the only ones that showed up. The event was run by another well known disc jockey named Sandy Beach who worked for WPOP's rival radio station WDRC. It was agreed that if we played extra we would get paid double our fee. This is one of the first sneaky showbiz deals we would encounter. Of course, nothing was written down, and of course, we didn't get paid extra. Once bitten twice shy. Also that winter we played New Year's Eve at The Lanes in Brewster, New York. The drinking age in Connecticut was 21, but only 18 in New York. Everyone in the band but me got toasted. Lots of angels in the snow that night. I drove us all home, 40 miles at the age of 16, very late at night and in the blowing snow.

    One of the steady gigs we had was playing The Hartford gay bar scene in downtown Hartford by the State Capitol. There was The Beef And Bourbon Steakhouse, The Haufbrau House, and The Asylum. Being tall, I passed for being 18 years old. We did so well we became the house band for The Asylum. They loved our name. The owners of the clubs and the audiences were all really super and there were never any problems. We never judged anyone and in turn they did not judge us. My mom would ask, where are you playing tonight and I'd reply, the fictitious Hartford High.

    At the end of the summer, we changed drummers. Bill Buckland was going to study engineering at UConn in Storrs Ct. He would be instrumental a few years later in telling me of a great band he had seen which eventually became the band New England. Our new drummer, Wally Adomovich, also from Bristol Ct., was a great addition to our sound. He was a terrific drummer and played with a flashy style. All was going along very well but we were about to learn a new lesson in showbiz about good and bad managers. Management 101.

Around this time Gary's car was up on blocks, as he had blown his transmission drag racing and didn't have the means to get it repaired. Gary's father was a big wig in the Connecticut Association of Ham Radio Operators. There was an upcoming convention coming up in a few months at Lake Compounce with over 1000 attendees signed up. With our new affiliation with Christopher Productions going along well, the convention was one of the few engagements Gary had to offer us in a long time. Lake Compounce was an amusement park in Southington, Connecticut. It was opened in 1846 and is the oldest continuously operating amusement park in the United States. Its huge ballroom saw the likes of The Tommy Dorsey Orchestra and Frank Sinatra. Also, every well-known country artist from the 50's and 60's played there. In the 80's, Milli Vanilli was broadcast live on MTV from there and it was the first public sign they were lip-syncing.

All of us had been there many times, having grown up in the area. We all agreed this would be a great gig for us with the possibility of selling lots of our records. Just before the event, two things happened simultaneously: Number one, we received a letter from our bank stating that we were missing two payments on our PA system loan. They were going to charge late fees. Number two, and very suspicious, was that Gary's car was back on the road, running smoothly and better than ever.

We went over well. Immediately after the band played its show at Lake Compounce, Jerry Talbot accused our manager, Gary Prez, of stealing from the band. Where were the missing payments to the bank as we had given them to Gary to pay the loan? Gary was so defensive and nervous that he combined the words stealing and thief together, blurting out, "Are you calling me a steef?" We thought this was hilarious and everyone joined in calling him a steef as we packed up our equipment. We retained ownership of the PA system and eventually paid off the loan. We continued without Gary.

It was my first lesson that sometimes situations aren't always what they appear to be. The excitement and lure of success is very emotional and you are in a state of mind to be taken advantage of. Research is the best policy in evaluating a deal. There are other times when you try as you may, you can never see something bad coming along. Trust is a fickle friend in the business of making music. I would make more misjudgments of deals and people.

In 1785, Robert Burns wrote a poem entitled "To A Mouse". It contains the famous quote "The best laid plans o` mice an` men gang aft agley." It translates to "The best laid plans of mice and men often go awry". The line suggests that no matter how carefully you plan things, they can still go wrong.

Up to mid 1968 I felt I was in control of my own destiny. I had the security of starting a successful band with my friends based at my house. It was the center of our world. I have never been a side man. All of the bands I've been in, whether the Insane, New England, or Alcatrazz, have all been bands that I helped launch from scratch. We were a group of guys sitting around a table saying, "let's start a band in our own vision and musical style." As John Lennon is quoted as saying, "Where are we going? To the top boys!" A democratic band must have a sense of loyalty and brotherhood to prevail in the musical marketplace– The band becomes family. All for one and one for all. Divorce can be ugly and expensive.

As my senior year was coming to a close, I was about to graduate high school in 1968. There are a lot of changes going on in the world. It was the time of the Vietnam War, the Chicago Democratic Convention, and riots in the streets. Richard Nixon was elected President and his term wound up in the Watergate Scandal with him resigning. Martin Luther King and Robert F. Kennedy were assassinated. Lyndon Johnson signed the Civil

Rights Act, and The Apollo 8 was the first manned orbit of the moon. Star Trek filmed the first interracial kiss on TV and George Romeo premiered The Night Of The Living Dead, the beginning of the zombie craze. Last but not least, the Big Mac was invented, along with stackable Pringles.

Bob Dylan sang "the times they are changing", and they sure were. Bill Buckland had left the band to go to college, and now we were losing our new drummer, Wally Adamovich, for the same reason. He said that if he was going to go to college, he was going to give up the drums to concentrate on his studies. The draft was in full swing. Billy Tomlin decided that he would join the Navy for 4 years rather than be drafted into the Army; he said he wanted to be a Navy pilot. The Navy had other ideas, and he was assigned to be an aircraft carrier flagman, considered one of the most dangerous jobs in the Navy. Jerry, Peter Brown, and I were now in a conundrum. It would take time to find a new drummer and guitarist, so we begin weighing our options.

The only band in town that we thought was competition for us was a band called Fate. They were a very talented three-piece band but never really played out much. The band consisted of Bob Mohr playing guitar and organ, And their bass player, Butch Hart, who had been in the Merrays. I used to listen to them at The Popular Restaurant when I was younger. The drummer was the young Larry Maringola, who was instrumental in my wanting to play an instrument.

I always thought he was the one from town that would go on to stardom.

The six of us had a meeting and talked about the possibility of merging forces. Two bands would be better as one, opening up new areas for us musically. Jerry Talbot would play lead guitar / vocals. Bob Mohr would play rhythm guitar / organ / vocals, Butch Hart would switch from bass to rhythm guitar / vocals, Peter Brown would be our organist/vocalist, Larry would be the drummer, and I would play bass and vocals.

We liked the band Traffic. It was decided to keep the one word name Fate rather than a band name starting with the word 'The', like The Insane. In addition, we now had two PA systems, 2 keyboard players and 2 guitarists. It was decided that we would practice at Bob Mohr's parents' house. They lived in a nice subdivision at the base of the Southington Mountain Ski Resort. Bob had graduated a year before and Butch was a bit older and had a full-time factory job. Larry was doing a good job of dropping out of school. Little did we know at the time that Bob would also get drafted. He chose the Navy and served honorably for four years as a Submariner.

The Insane had done well, selling most of the 500 copies of our record. We didn't sell them all, but we turned a profit on them. We now had a set list of about 60 songs between both bands and rehearsals began right away, but not at the frequency of our time at my house on Liberty Street. I was approached by the committee of students at school who were responsible for putting on our Class Day Celebration. Would my band be up for playing? The 1968 graduating class of Southington High School chose to have the class day party at a country club in Orange Connecticut, 40 Miles away. All the students would go by bus. I was allowed to drive my van full of equipment. We also had a car for the band members. The Class Day gig was a lot of fun. Since most of our gigs the previous year and a half were out of town, most of my classmates had never seen the band play live. We got a rousing reception playing as a quartet. Butch had to work and couldn't come, and Peter was nowhere to be found. I even made peace with our Vice President, Mr. Gasecki, who had expelled me numerous times over the last two years for the length of my hair and the dress code. The whole event was super and a great closing to my 4 years in high school.

"No one is so brave that he is not disturbed by something unexpected." Julius Caesar said that in 49 BC.

As we started to set up for rehearsal a week later, my world came crashing down. Peter Brown was a no-show and would disappear on us altogether, Jerry and Bob informed me that they felt four guys could earn more than a six man band, therefore I was out, leaving Bob, Jerry, Butch, and Larry to carry on together. I was devastated and never saw this coming. After the initial shock of being left out of the lineup I couldn't believe that all this was done by my supposed friends behind my back. The conversation was short and it didn't take long for me to pack my gear in my van. I gave no alternative scenarios. No pleading to stay. I was blindsided and deeply wounded, especially by my friend Jerry, as we had done a lot together. I'll always remember driving down the road, pulling over, and crying to myself. Poor me.

It only took a few minutes to charge back up and declare in defiance that I would strike out into the world on my own, showing those guys a thing or two. As I look back on that day, it's one of the best things that ever happened to me. I had enough anger and chutzpah to carry on for years. Fate became a band that would only play an occasional gig now and then. We eventually patched up our friendship, however, which exists to this day.

The great bluesman Robert Johnson wrote Crossroad in 1936. He sang, "I went down to the crossroad and fell down on my knees". Like him, I had come to the crossroads of happenstance and predestination. They would lay ahead of me as I thought and rethought the direction I would take, planning my next move.

I had enrolled myself at Mattatuck Community College in Waterbury, Connecticut. Aside from studying history and a jazz appreciation class, it wasn't cutting it. I knew that what I needed to do was immerse myself in the music scene. All I thought about was bass and spent my time at my parents' house wood shedding. There wasn't much going on in the local scene and I had given up on pursuing another band. One of the memories I have of this time is to have seen so many great bands play live with the original members. I made it my mission to explore what made them popular. Most of them only had their first albums out. Jethro Tull played at an Asian restaurant called The Stone Balloon in New Haven, and I saw The Chicago Transit Authority. The original Steppenwolf played at The Bushnell Auditorium in Hartford. Their guitarist, Michael Monarch, looked like Keith Richards and played like Jeff Beck. They played through a wall of Rickenbacker amplifiers. The band was inspiring and I hoped someday to be in a band like that. A few years later I would find myself sitting in a London hotel room with Michael and singer / drummer Jon Hyde, playing songs like Memphis and joining their new band, which was the precursor to the Led Zeppelin backed band, Detective.

After seeing Ronnie Wood playing a new Fender Telecaster bass with The Jeff Beck Group, I decided I had to have one. I should have kept my 60's Precision bass but no one knew then how valuable it would become someday. I put some money down to order one and went to Manny's Music in New York City. The store manager, Henry, explained there was a slight problem. There were two orders but only one bass came in. There was a customer walking around the store with ultra flashy clothes and wild hair. My friend Billy Hayes said he thought it was Mitch Mitchell, drummer of the Jimi Hendrix band. Henry called Mitch over explaining how we both wanted the same bass and that we should work it out between us. Mitch was extremely friendly and explained that he just wanted a bass to fool around on and that he had no problem getting something else. I couldn't believe it. He said take the bass and I wish you well. We returned home smiling and I had my first brand new electric bass. My conversation with Mitch was inspiring and very influential. I couldn't believe that someone of his success would take the time out to befriend a couple of young fans. He took the edge off stardom and spoke to us as neighbors. I hoped that one day I would be able to inspire young musicians and music fans in a similar way.

The summer of 1969 was pivotal for the amount of music I heard live. My friends and I went to the Atlantic City Pop Festival, The Newport Jazz Festival, and Woodstock all in four weeks. I saw most of the 90 bands that performed and took mental notes of what I liked about the music and their performances. Seeing The Who, Sly and The Family Stone, Santanna, Mountain, Johnny Winter, B.B. King, Jimi Hendrix, Led Zeppelin, The Jeff Beck Group, etc. etc. was an electric, memorable experience. I felt that this was the education I needed.

The following school year, my friend, Charlie Early, and I drove to Boston almost every weekend and saw more great bands playing live, like Humble Pie at The Boston Tea Party. Our friend, Donna Ferrucci, was going to the The Art Institute and I began making friends with dozens of students and musicians. That summer my friend, Patric Nagle, and I hitchhiked from Connecticut to Northern California in four days. We went to visit our good friend Peter Maynell, who had left Southington and moved to the Mendocino area of Northern California. Patrick and I spent three months camping like Robinson Crusoe along the Navarro River where it flows into the Pacific Ocean. It was a relaxing adventure and gave me time to think things out for the next part of my life. I knew I wanted to play bass in a great band and make original music. While in San Francisco I got to see Mott The Hoople open for The Quicksilver Messenger Service at the Fillmore West, along with Lee Stevens of Blue Cheer. As summer came to a close Patrick decided that he wanted to stay in Humboldt County, Ca. and pursue the country lifestyle. I yearned for the big city lights and flew back east.

My plan was finalized. I knew which road to take at this fork in life. I had traveled east and west across the country. I didn't particularly care for the San Francisco music scene. Not being a native New Yorker I knew that moving south to Manhattan without much money would be precarious, if not downright crazy. My plan was to leave school and move north to that city on the bay, Boston Massachusetts. From there I felt I could re-launch myself in a city that has had a great music scene since 1620 and beyond.

There is something exciting about moving to a new place. Old items left behind and new ones found. How about you? Did you move around with your parents or in your adult years? I lived in a total of 7 homes with my parents and the total number of addresses I've had on my own is over two dozen. Living in different places gives a broader look at the world. It's true that people want the same things all over the world for their families, regardless of language, race, or religion.

I was moving on up to the mighty City of Boston. Boston is ruled by two sacred institutions, The Red Sox and The J. Geils Band. Dissing either one can get you in real trouble. The city is on the Atlantic ocean and has over 40 colleges in the metro area. It's estimated that there are over 250,000 students all living in a few square miles of the Charles River. This translates to a myriad of bars, clubs and schools to play at. The musical talent pool is at the top of the list with schools like Berklee College of Music, Boston Conservatory, Harvard, and Boston University. Lots of great musicians and gigs. Before moving to my new apartment, I stayed with our friend Donna Ferrucci in the Back Bay. The Back Bay is predominantly students living in small apartments that haven't been renovated since the 1940s. Parking, like most modern cities, is at a premium. Boston has the oldest subway system in the U. S., however, and makes for a very walkable city.

I had to wait a month to move into my new place due to the lease running from September to September. My two new roommates, Caleb Fulham and Nick Cameron, would also arrive then. One afternoon Donna and I came home to find the veneer of the apartment door cracked. Upon further inspection, the door was forced open, the stereo and the albums were stacked in the middle of the room for a second visit as Donna's sewing machine was stolen and so was my Telecaster bass and Spanish guitar. I had chiseled out a space on the body of my new bass to add a second pickup as I didn't like how the bass sounded. The thieves never came back. Nor did they get the Telecaster bass pickguard which I had removed. If you ever see a 1968 Telecaster bass with 2 pickups in vintage cream and a maple neck, let me know.

The following week. I made another trip to Manny's Music in New York City as well as a pawn shop on 6th Avenue. The pawnshop looked normal from the outside, but they had a room upstairs jammed with guitars and basses. Getting upstairs took a lot of haggling with the owners. Something like this, The owner: "Why should I show you upstairs, you have no money," Me: "Yes, I do." Owner: "Show it to me." Me: "I'm not showing anything until I can look upstairs." Upstairs was a guitarist's dream. The room was split into sections and there were signs saying Fender, Gibson, Gretsch, Guild, etc. An easy 200 instruments, with violins, cellos, and upright bases in between. I found a rare early 1950s Gibson EB -1 bass. I knew it would have been a major investment and worth big money someday. It was like the bass Jack Bruce and Felix Pappalardi played. It was the kind of bass you didn't want to take out of the house. I could have spent all day there picking through the cases. In hindsight, I wish I could have taken photos of what I saw.

Not wanting to make a decision yet, I headed over to Manny's Music. There, staring at me, was a 1965 L-series Fender Jazz Bass in Lake Placid blue. It had a Precision Bass neck on it and had a used price tag of $140.00. I had $350.00 total. I bought the bass with its original case and was also able to buy a used Marshall Major 200 watt amplifier as well .Again, my new bass would be worth over $10,000.00 one day. I have played that bass and traveled everywhere in the world with it. It's on most of the albums that I've recorded. When I moved into my apartment, I sanded off the blue paint and primer right down to the bare alderwood and put a clear lacquer on it with a brush. There was a crack in the headstock near the first fret and I shoved Elmer's glue into it. I've never had to redo it .One day I noticed that the Telecaster pickguard that I had would fit over the Jazz body with some slight modification. I like the look of it covering the horn. I turned on our gas stove and took a red-hot butter knife to the edges that needed trimming. Some light sanding took off some rough spots, and it has remained the same since. I added a Badass bridge to it during our recording sessions for "Disturbing The Peace" by Alcatrazz in the fall of 1984.

There are no problems, only opportunities. I had turned a bad situation into a good one. The Jazz Bass to me is far superior in sound and playability than the reissue Telecaster. I had met a catastrophe head-on and came out victorious. Now I was ready to start playing bass and making music around the world.

The Boston Phoenix was an alternative newspaper equivalent to The Village Voice in New York City. It had city politics, upcoming events and a classified ad section in the back with listings of the clubs in Boston and who was playing. There was Passim's Coffee House and Jack's in Cambridge. In Boston it was The Groggery, Katy's, Lucifer's, Buratty's and The Rathskeller. The Rat had a history of bands playing there like The Police and The

Talking Heads. In 1981 when they remodeled the club, New England played on the reopening night. There was always something going on with over 32 bars and restaurants in the Boston area.

I answered an ad for a bass player and found myself at a house in the nearby city of Malden. I met guitarist songwriter Greg Chansky and his younger brother, Paul, who played keyboards. The former dining room of their parents' house was filled with rare guitars, a Hammond C-3 organ that once belonged to The Boston Tea Party, and Marshall amplifiers. It made me suspicious at first until I heard Greg sing and play some of his original songs. His voice was deep like Cat Stevens and his songs were very creative like Joni Mitchell. Paul was an accomplished piano player, and together they were looking to form a band. We sat around and talked about our mutual influences like Jeff Beck and Terry Reid. We played records and talked about our favorite music. Greg was anxious to get out of his parents' house and Paul was just finishing school.

It was decided that we would place an ad for a drummer in The Boston Phoenix. A drummer from Washington DC answered the ad. In walked a killer drummer named Barry Brandt. He and his bass player friend Donnie Jones had come North following a singer named Ralph Mormon. Ralph had joined the Boston band Daddy Warbux. He would one day sing for the Joe Perry Project and Savoy Brown. Donnie and Barry would go on to form the group Angel with Punky Meadows, Frank Di Mino, and Greg Guiffria. Barry said he was open to joining up with us. Donnie was not happy about that and went back to D.C., later changing his name to Mickie Jones.

Greg had a friend named Mark Berland from New York City who played jazz fusion guitar like John McGlaughlin. We thought it was a great concept, having two guitarists, one rock and one jazzy. He also knew and introduced us to a lead singer of the local band

Autumn Stone. They were East Boston's version of The Faces. Frank Di Mino was his name, and he sang like Roger Daltrey of The Who. We thought we had the winning combination of guys to play Greg's original songs along with his great voice. We weren't going to be a Top 40 band but a band that would get a record deal on a major label playing original music. The next idea was to find a house where we could all live and rehearse like madmen.

The search for houses to rent began. All of this was funded by Greg and myself, but I really believed in the music, so I wasn't too worried about the expense. A friend of mine, Ruth Bitten, needed to get home to her family in New Jersey for her father's birthday. Her father was editor of the Trenton Times and we decided to give her a ride home in Greg's Cadillac hearse. Maybe we would find a farm or a house to rent in the surrounding area. We didn't find anything after a week and realized we were six hours drive from Boston. On the way home we stopped for gas in the town of Storrs Connecticut, very close to U. Conn. While in the store we found an ad for a house to rent nearby. We found a beautiful house in the quiet rolling hills of Coventry on Silver Lake Road. Our only neighbor was Nathan Hale's Historic Homestead down the street. We could raise hell here 24 hours a day and it was only a ninety-minute drive to Boston.

And so it began. I thought of the irony of coming back to Connecticut. Only myself Greg, and Barry, made the move. The other three got cold feet and didn't want to participate. We didn't have much furniture, just four Marshall stacks and Barry's Ludwig drum kit with a 26 inch kick drum. I would go out in the morning through the woods and sing lyrics at the top of my voice like The Beatles "Go To Get You Into My Life". Barry would be in the house playing along to Edgar Winter's White Trash album at full volume. As the days went on, Greg kept going deeper into manic depression. He was always having headaches and not feeling good. Nothing got finished or finalized with the music. Everything would be better if this or that happened. Greg was like Atlas, carrying the weight of the world on his shoulders. Never appreciating what we did have, always second guessing everything with no conclusions.

On a good note, my friend Bill Buckland from The Insane was going to UConn and paid us a visit. He was floored by Barry's drumming and the music we were playing. There was a very good venue nearby called The Shaboo, and he told us of an amazing band he'd seen there. He said that they had big drums, big keyboards, and a big bass sound with a lead singer, but no guitar player. Every song was long and well played in the style of progressive rock. The band was from North Carolina, and they were called Fat Back. This was a monumental piece of information as we'll see a few years later.

With Christmas and Hanukkah coming up Greg, Barry and myself decided to call it quits. Barry went back to Washington, DC and Greg and I returned to Boston. My 21st birthday was coming up and although I lost some money, I learned some new financial lessons in life. I was still eager to play original music that I enjoyed and could be proud of.

Upon returning to Boston, I was able to move in with my good friends Jim and Jack Wiener. Identical twins and both really talented artists from Allentown Pennsylvania. Jack is in the book, "200 years of American Art", and Jim taught ceramics and computer art at The Museum School Of Fine Art. They were able to get a 5 bedroom 3 bath apartment in Brookline's Coolidge Corner neighborhood at the time when renting to long-haired tenants was frowned upon. Everyone in the house was in art school. I eventually got the master bedroom with its own bathroom. It was a time of art, music, and a lot of laughter. Things were looking up. These were the days of no internet or cell phones. Everyone carried a phone book, and pay phones were everywhere. There was one phone in the house to be shared by all.

I again answered an ad in the Phoenix for a bass player and met Tom Lewis and Sydney Clarke, both of whom were enrolled in The Berklee College of Music. Tom was a left-handed drummer from New Jersey and one day would play for The Harry James Orchestra. Sydney was an excellent guitarist also from Connecticut. Their friend Roy played piano in the music program at Boston University. We wanted to be very musical and were in awe of The John McLaughlin Orchestra. I had a lead singer friend named Scott Anderson. His favorite band was the group Free. We all met together and discussed how we could put a heavily orchestrated jazz rock band behind a minimalist vocalist. Our set list grew, as we added songs by Brian Auger's Oblivion Express, John McLaughlin, and assorted artists like Argent. I preferred leaning more to rock than jazz but it was a great learning experience. We were anxious to show off what we could do musically.

The subject of the band name came up and Scott said he had a suggestion. Recently he'd lost a musician friend in a fatal accident coming home from a gig in New Hampshire on Interstate 93. While driving a Volkswagen bus loaded with gear, his friend was killed by a runaway truck. He had told Scott a few weeks before of a dream he had of killer oats coming down from Canada and taking over America. Hearing that story we all agreed that the name of our band would be Killer Oats in his honor. We rehearsed around Tom, Syd, and Roy's school schedules. We rehearsed at Scott's house in Norwood and Roy's grandmother's basement in Needham. We actually did some 4 track recordings there with microphones suspended from the furnace ducts that I still have. It was a beautiful summer in Boston and we played some clubs around town.

Unfortunately, I sensed that the other guys were not that committed to the band, as they were working towards graduating from college. Our eclectic set of music wasn't endearing us to the nightclub owners. The manager of Katys, Frankie Melga, told us we sucked because we refused to play Brown Sugar by The Rolling Stones. We told him that's what jukeboxes were for, we were musicians, not copy robots. Needless to say, we didn't work there again. With fall coming in and a new school year coming up I didn't see a great future for Killer Oats in the Boston club scene. The guys were great and the music was cool to play but I decided the commitment was only 50%. I started asking myself what I really wanted. What would make me very happy? What was the next step in my musical odyssey? I knew the answer all the time and now it was time to make a move.

The Vietnam war was winding down and I no longer needed to worry about the draft. I told the draft board that I was left-handed but played bass right-handed. They said that's screwed up and gave me a 1-Y draft status, In Case Of National Emergency Only. The first half is not true, but the second half is. I was against the war, not wanting to help the French retain their colony. Richard Nixon was beginning a second term as president and finally ended the Vietnam war and the draft.

I said goodbye to my bandmates and had a new sense of freedom to do whatever I wanted. I told my friends Jack and Jim that I was moving out and arranged to leave my Ampeg SVT bass amp and a few things with them. Time to really stick out my neck and do something I always wanted to do musically. Most of my friends said my plan was very cool and some of them said I was crazy. I was moving to London, England with not much money and zero connections. I figured hell, I can always come back.

In 1783, the treaty of Paris officially ended the American Revolution and recognized significant Western Territory expansion. It also agreed on fishing rights and access to the Mississippi river. It set the boundary of the Northwest Territories and the border of the U.S. and Canada. The generous concessions of the British were designed to open up new markets for British merchants without military cost to The Crown.

Growing up in Connecticut and living in Boston I was surrounded by stories of George Washington's blue coats against the red coats of King George II. Seeing England someday was on my list of things to do.

There had been another British invasion of music in the late 60s, and it continues today. Post-World War II English musicians began listening to the American GI's rhythm and blues records. They loved what they heard and began to emulate what they were listening to. They put an Anglo spin on the music, combining the blues with their British accents. Hence the birth of The Rolling Stones, The Animals, The Beatles, John Mayall, and many others. The guitar took a prominent position in the songs launching the careers of Eric Clapton, Jeff Beck, Jimmy Page, Alvin Lee, and a host of other British greatshers.

The music went from pop arrangements to the 12 bar blues format. This was the music that caught my ear as a teenager. It had a harder edge and seductive lyrics. There were radio stations playing R&B music in the U.S., but they were relegated to the back of the pack behind the white pop music. To buy these records meant going into the inner city neighborhoods of big cities.

I had grown up in post-world War II America. I had never heard of John Lee Hooker, Robert Johnson, or the great Willie Dixon until I heard the English bands' versions. Even the term rock and roll came from the world of R&B talking about sex and betrayal. I learned what a back door man was and what a voodoo child was. They were a threat to white conservative values and they called it the devil's music. It was derived from the call and response songs of the laborers in the fields, played on cheap guitars, harmonicas and out of tune pianos. Greg Chansky and I had ventured down into Georgia and Louisiana on our trip to Trenton, New Jersey. We saw at first hand the homes of sharecroppers and the remains of slavery life. Needless to say, it was eye-opening to see it for real.

Now I was interested in finding the source of this English Blues Invasion. What made Liverpool different from Birmingham, Sheffield or London? Why did The Rolling Stones smirk at The Beatles being from Liverpool? Jerry Talbot's brother, Mike, was stationed in Germany and brought home an album we loved. It was an Irish band called Taste with a guitarist named Roy Gallagher. Who were these guys? Where was all this fire and terrific guitar playing coming from? It was inspiring to me, and I had to find out what shaped this music.

Also I was very mesmerized with the classical rock style of King Crimson's record, The Court Of The Crimson King, with their use of a keyboard called a Mellotron and medieval lyrics. I dug The Nice with Keith Emerson, playing songs from West Side Story, along with Spooky Tooth, yes, and The Moody Blues orchestrated sound. I loved the Move's Night Of Fear and the Small Faces, Itchycoo Park. No one played as fast and grinding as Deep Purple's Highway Star.

I had just turned 21 and felt it was the right time to go to London. I had seen the Haight Ashbury scene in San Francisco and knew it wasn't for me. Why not try and join some English bands and see and learn new things? I felt I had nothing to lose and it was time to strike while the iron was hot. I bought a ticket on a red eye flight between Boston's Logan Airport and London's Heathrow Airport. With no contacts other than some advice of a few clubs to visit from some friends who had been there, I was off.

I flew into the dark eastern sky with my trusty Jazz bass and a small suitcase, not knowing what to expect in the English music scene. As I flew eventually into the rising sun, I had been talking to a fellow passenger. He was a history professor and was going to the Himalayas to ponder the mysteries of life. I figured my quest would be a bit simpler. He was going to visit friends in Scotland and suggested we get a hotel in London for one night and part ways the next day. I agreed. My interview with customs was a precursor of difficulties to come. They asked where I was going and I said to music college. They asked did I have any paperwork? I answered no and got a visa for one month. Cheers to you too, gentlemen.

I bought a copy of Melody Maker and after figuring out what the pips of the payphone were, I called a bass player ad. It was Mungo Jerry, who had a hit with the song "In the Summertime". They said come to this particular pub at 5 pm. in London and I said sure.

That never happened. We searched the paper for hotels and picked a bed and breakfast. It happened to be in the Notting Hill Gate area which, as fate would have it, was pretty much in the center of the music scene. It was not far from Island Records studios or Abbey Road studios. Kensington High Street and the trendy fashion scene were also nearby.

Just as we were approaching the bed and breakfast hotel that we had booked, a young man my age was walking towards us. He looked like Marc Bolan of T. Rex, like the epitome of Jumping Jack Flash. He had glitter eye makeup, two scarves, rings of necklaces, assorted bracelets, two belts on remade jeans, and stars on this platform boots. I thought he was either a big poser or someone that was talented. He stopped and asked if that was a bass I was carrying. I wanted to say, no it's a xylophone, as I bit my lip and said yes. He introduced himself as Michael Corby and that he was a guitarist recently sacked from the Susie Quatro Band. He then stunned me by saying he was starting a new band with Spooky Tooth guitarist Luther Grovesnor. I had not slept a wink on the plane and this all felt surreal. He said they were looking for a bass player. Would I like to go to Luther's flat the next day and meet him. All I kept thinking was Spooky Tooth. He said Spooky Tooth, wow! I tried to remain cool while my body was shaking with exhaustion and excitement and mumbled something like, sure.

Michael mentioned that there was going to be a press party that evening for a band called The Pink Fairies at a trendy burger restaurant named The Great American Disaster, one of London's first hamburger places. Would I like to go? I had known or heard of hundreds of bands, but never the Pink Fairies. I stowed my bass at the hotel and went along with him. I went to the new restaurant, The Great American Disaster, with the likes of Mia Farrow, Warren Beatty, Andre Previn, and Twiggy for customers. The Fairies were raucous, political anarchists, playing loud rock music like the MC5 from Detroit. Their name was short for The Pink Fairies Motorcycle Club and All Star Rock and Roll Band. They had recently played The Isle of Wight Rock Festival. Guess who was at the party? The MC5. They were all friends. I was talking to their guitarist, Wayne Kramer, and he invited me to the back hallway. A friend pulled out some cocaine and offered it to me. I had done some drugs before, but not coke. Now I was awake for a full 24 hours and beyond. I figured I'll sleep when I die. Needless to say it was a happening party with many music business-people in attendance.

The next day my professor friend checked out of the hotel headed for Scotland and the Himalayas. I stayed at the hotel for a week longer. I began going around London and learning all things English like counting money and the subway system with Michael. I bought new clothes, not wanting to look like an American tourist. No "Hi, I'm from the U.S" written across my chest for me. He said I could stay across the street in a building on Westbourne Grove. The town house had been taken over by squatters. He said they had room, why pay for a hotel? The Fairies' drummer, Russel, was staying there. It was not uncommon for their road crew to arrive midday and take Russel to rehearsal into the van lying prone on a stretcher.

Michael had a rehearsal studio at King's Cross and I met his French drummer friend, Roland. Roland's dad was a French junior ambassador to the U.S., and they had lived in Washington, D.C. Roland knew of Barry Brandt and Punky Meadows. I wasn't keen on playing in a trio but went along to see where things led. Roland didn't seem too motivated to me. Michael seemed to know a lot about the cogs of the music business and was constantly hustling recording studios for free recording time. He talked a big game and had a friend who managed a band called Streak, the precursor to The Arrows. Their guitarist, Jay Hooker, was married to Judy Garland's daughter, Lorna Luft. Michael, their manager, and I went to one of their rehearsals. We drove to Bermondsey, to the docks of East London. There, in an old row of warehouses, an intercom button was pushed and we drove into the building. When we got out of the car, I saw it was ultra modern inside with the best in production gear. It was The Rolling Stones' rehearsal complex. Damn! I was introduced to people and kept a low profile. I listened to the guys rehearse. They were very professional and friendly. Great guys. I would meet Jake a few years later at a party in Bill Aucoin's (my future manager) N.Y.C. home. Michael kept saying I was his dream bass player for the new band he had in mind. I knew exactly the style he was talking about, but I wasn't sure if we could do it together.

Another time we were at Warner Brothers Records executive Ian Samwell's house. He was busy releasing an album for their artist Linda Lewis. We watched Top Of The Pops at his home one night on television, with a few other people. Michael was going on about his opinions of what was good and bad. A fellow with short hair, round, wire rimmed glasses, dressed in black, was sitting quietly next to me. Michael spun around and asked him what band he was in. The guy quietly responded, King Crimson. It was Robert Fripp! I cringed and once more I was glad I wasn't shooting off my mouth like Sir Corby. He had a way of stirring things up. I began to distance myself. Michael would appear again in a few years. That story is coming up soon.

Confidence is a fickle friend. Do you have confidence right now or is it something that comes in and out of your life? Is it an ability that you can summon up at a snap of the fingers, or a crash course taken to control your insecurities? Everyone deals with it in different ways and strategies. Up to this point in my life, behind my bravado were certain questions of success that played ping pong in my mind. I didn't know that many of my fears were about to be vanquished. I owe that to a very special person.

Spooky Tooth is one of my all-time favorite bands. I loved Mike Harrison's smokey voice and Greg Ridley's beyond solid bass playing. Luther Grosvenor's guitar solo of wild abandon on the song "Evil Woman" is one of the best solos in rock music bar none. The band would go through lineup changes down the road but the lineup of Spooky Two was the one for me. The fact they didn't reach maximum stardom is a true tragedy of the music business. They had it all as far as I'm concerned, but it just wasn't in the cards.

Michael Corby was correct that he and Luther were talking about doing something together. By the time I got to England, Spooky Tooth had broken up and gone separate ways. They began recording solo albums while bassist Greg Ridley went off with Steve Marriott and Peter Frampton to form Humble Pie. Keyboardist Gary Wright, the American in the group, had a major hit in due time with the song "Dream Weaver". Luther released Under The Skies and Mike Harrison released Smokestack Lightning, both on Island Records. Mr. Corby and I took the tube down to Putney. We went around to Luther's flat and he opened the door. I had a Meeting Elvis Moment. With a big smile Luther welcomed us in and was very friendly. He had been living in Spain and the flat was furnished in a Spanish, Moroccan style with no furniture other than big pillows, carpets, and tapestries. It was actually very comfortable. Luthers's wife, Gita, was a Swedish model who had just finished an ad campaign for a major chocolate company. She was also very pleasant.

Michael began telling Luther of the people he had spoken to who were willing to invest in a new band and that would pay for recording time in a studio to get things rolling. I was introduced as a bass player friend with some experience who had recently come from the States, and that we had been playing together for a short time. Luther played us some tracks from his new album and they sounded really good. We decided nothing could be done until we had investor support to fund rehearsals etc.. We came back a few times and Luther told me to feel free to pop by for a visit any time.

One day I found myself alone with Luther and he asked me for my assessment of the project Michael was trying to put together. Little did I know that Luther had recently recorded the slide guitar solo on Stealers Wheel's hit song :Stuck In The Middle With You". He told me they had made him an offer to join the band full time and what would I do if I was him? I didn't feel any betrayal to Michael by telling Luther, if I was him, I would definitely take the Stealers Wheel gig. As far as the Michael band was concerned, in all honesty it was still nothing but conversation. I'll never know if my two cents of advice was heeded or not, but Luther joined Stealers Wheel.

Luther had a very good friend who lived upstairs named Arthur Belcher along with his wife Margaret. They were also from Carlisle in The Lakes District of England, where Luther and Mike Harrison came from. He played sax and piano and everyone got along fine. They liked my American stories and told people I was from Texas, as I was over six feet tall.

In the meantime, Arthur had written songs that he wanted to record and asked my help doing it. Arthur had a 4 track recorder. We laid down piano and bass tracks. We used tambourines for the lack of drums, and wooden matchstick boxes for shakers– which had 2 sounds, lengthwise and edgewise. Luther would come home from his rehearsals and lay down acoustic guitar tracks from a funky collection of guitars hanging on the walls of his living room. Luther was very supportive of my playing and I was able to relax and enjoy myself and the music we were making. We had great fun and I was allowed to stay overnight with both couples like a visiting relative. At Christmas I drove up to Carlisle with everyone and met their families. I chuckled as they had to psyche themselves up for a six hour car ride like we were driving to Mars. I had a really good time, as the day after Christmas is Boxing Day when all the sports games and drinking are done. The day after that was my birthday.

    Mike Harrison and Mike Kelly would stop by and hang out, listening to Arthur and Luther's 4 track tapes. I learned that they were all influenced by the Nashville studio musician groups Barefoot Jerry and Area Code 615. Wayne Moss was one of their big heroes. I was amazed that these rock guys wanted to be down home country guys. One of the songs I played bass on called "Friend" was re-recorded in Nashville on Mike Harrison's album Rainbow Rider in 1975. I listen to it now and I can still hear the matchboxes.

    Through Luther's support and friendship, I developed a great sense of confidence and inner security. I felt like I had passed a test to play major league music. Luther went on to play with Mott The Hoople with the stage name Aerial Bender. Later, I saw his band Widowmaker and got to hang out with him in Providence Rhode Island on the 1978 Ted Nugent / Foreigner Tour. I shall always be grateful for his kind words and hospitality.

    The thrill of victory, the agony of defeat. Is there a job application or audition that terrified you? Perhaps show business has more ups and downs than the real world. Hero to zero overnight. Like any job, being in the right place at the right time is imperative, and then you must have the goods. Average actors can be marketed for only so long but real talent endures. The rejection of auditioning makes and breaks some people. Sometimes not getting the gig is the best thing that ever happened to you, leaving you an opening for something else coming your way.

    My next endeavor was going north to Wolverhampton in the Midlands. It was a gray day with rain pouring down. I went to the address of a small theater. The audition was for the group Trapeze. A very good three piece band that had records out and was touring the world. Their bass player, Glenn Hughes, had decided to move over to second guitar and was the band's lead singer. They wanted to add a new bass player. Their setup was very professional. In the small hall they had their entire stage gear and full P.A. setup. I was not familiar with their music, but I knew who they were. I was given a cassette player with three of their original songs. One thing missing was the bass tracks. Nothing to go on. I was told to give the songs a listen and when I felt good about the arrangements and chord changes, let them know. I said OK and took a seat in the back.

There were about 30 people there and they were auditioning someone on the stage at full volume. Not the best way for me to figure out someone's music by ear in 20 minutes. I thought this is as good as it's going to get and I said I was ready. Up on the stage I went and I was greeted very cordially. I plugged into an amplifier and off we went. As we played the songs, I had Glenn standing next to me and calling out chords like E minor, A minor, E major. Not the most relaxing situation I've ever played. I suggested perhaps we could jam along on something for a few minutes. They thought that was a good idea and the three of us played a funky riff in the vein of Stevie Wonder's song "Superstition". All well and good. I was driven to the train station by their manager. He gave me two of their lps for a call back. He said I had done very well and I was in the top three of contenders. Two weeks passed and no phone call. Later on I read that Glenn Hughes had joined Deep Purple and Trapeze had decided on a local bass player who didn't have immigration problems like me.

Usually in those days you never saw an ad divulging much about who the artist was. They usually read Name Band or must be able to travel extensively. While I was flipping through yet another copy of Melody Maker, I kept telling myself to hang in there. Good things happen to those who wait, blah, blah, blah .I didn't know how long I could stay in England and I wanted to make the most of it. It was up to me to make things happen, and that involves a lot of wishful thinking.

As I flipped through the ads, one caught my eye in a major way. It read: ex Steppenwolf guitarist seeks rock bass player and rock drummer. Whoa, I thought to myself in disbelief. I thought back to seeing Steppenwolf play in Hartford a few years before. That was the kind of ad opportunity I was looking for. Could it be the same guitarist I had seen back then? Figuring I had nothing to lose I picked up the phone, crossed my fingers, and made the call. Sure enough a voice answered and I was talking to Michael Monarch, the original Steppenwolf guitarist and the guy who played on the song "Born To Be Wild." I didn't know what to say. When he heard I was an American, he asked me what state I was from. I replied, Connecticut. He then told me that he and his partner had come to London to hire English band mates. I didn't know what to say to that. Then he seemed to change his mind, saying I could come over to his hotel that evening and we could see how things went.

His hotel was near Hyde Park and I met Jon Hyde, who was a great drummer but wanted to be a frontman vocalist. Jon had played drums for the very popular band The Prince and The Paupers in Boston, before relocating to Los Angeles. We sat around the hotel room and played songs like "Memphis" by Johnny Rivers and we talked about music. Michael and Jon had just released an album in Los Angeles under the band name Hocus Pocus. Their style was like The Faces with Jeff Beck on lead guitar. Great record. I stayed a couple of hours and Michael said he'd call in the morning. I went home more than ecstatic that it all felt good. The next day, no phone call. Next week, no call. Oh well

I thought and then my phone rang. It was Michael. He said they had found an English rhythm section but they felt it wasn't working out. Would I come down? Sure thing.

I went to a rehearsal studio down on Kings Road. I met the drummer they chose, Herman Rarebell, who was a German. He played like John Bonham. Things got strange as Jon was telling Herman how to play drums and Michael wanted me to play with a pick. Note to bass players: learn how to play with a pick AND your fingers. I started out playing with a thumb pick when I first began playing bass, however, I quickly switched to my fingers. As time went by, Herman and I went out to the clubs at night to see bands, but Michael and Jon had brought their girlfriends and chose to stay at home. We were doing alright, but the bonding didn't feel right.

Herman declared, Gary, rock is three things, pointing to his head, heart, and crotch. He said, is here, is here, is here. I agreed. Herman said that he had met a really hot guitar player at the Marquee club and that we should start our own band. Sure, let's give that a go.

My replacement was Prescott Niles, who came in from L.A. He would later play on the song "My Sharona" with The Knack. A few years later, in L.A., he and I would both audition for a sixteen year old supposed wunderkind guitarist from Chicago managed by his mother. We laughed together and didn't think the hype was warranted. Neither one of us got the gig, if there ever was one.

Michael and John went on to form the group Detective, backed by Jimmy Page of Led Zeppelin, with Tony Kay from Yes, lead vocalist Michael Des Barre of Silverhead, bassist Bobby Pickett from Sugar Loaf, and Jon on drums. To this day, we're all still friends.

Now the audition process was going to reverse itself. It was now time that I was the one who would place an ad in Melody Maker. My bandmates and I would be the ones making choices of who to add to our new band. Herman and I had a vision of how we wanted our band to be, similar to Michael and Jon's quest. We wanted to be a hard-hitting bluesy rock band that was interesting to listen to and fun to see live on stage. Easier said than done. The right musicians must have a combination of talent, personality, and stage presence. In your mind's eye you see the image of the person or persons you're looking for. If it happens, it's usually a form of magic. Some bands are very stylized and that adds to the difficulty of the search.

The best example of this is the story of Ian Stewart and The Rolling Stones. He was a founding member of the band and played piano on all of The Rolling Stones records for the first six years. Unfortunately, he was a large guy and management felt he didn't fit into the image of the band. He would not be in any press photos or perform at any live appearances. Would The Beatles be different if there were five of them? Did the fans care if it was The Dave Clark 5 or The Dave Clark 6? Andrew Loog Oldham felt six was too many to concentrate on. Ian accepted that fact and for the next 20 years, he remained in The Stones camp as family, playing a support role.

Herman had been to the Marquee club and seen an American band that had a very special guitarist. His name was David Cooper, and he went under the name of D. h. Cooper. He was cool onstage and played with fire. His band from New York City had managed to book a few shows in London. Herman told David he should quit his band and toss his lot in with us. To the dismay of his bandmates, he quit the band. It made for bad vibes, as David owned some of the band gear as well, further putting them in a bind.

I went around to meet David at the flat he shared with his girlfriend Catherine. They would eventually get married and David would not move back to The States. He was an extremely talented guitarist and had a number of original songs he had written. He had a great sense of humor and we all got along instantly. We talked about music direction and goals into the night. He had grown up in Westchester County, New York not far from me in Connecticut. We bonded and felt we had a lot in common.

We arranged to book initial rehearsal time at ACM Studios on Kings Road where Herman and I had played with Michael Monarch and Jon Hyde. Our instrumental rehearsals went well and we were pleased at the noise we were making. Unfortunately, studio rental time was not cheap. Herman was living at Hampton Court, Hampshire House, Richmond Surrey, at Ray Galton's home, formerly owned by Henry VIII. Ray and his partner Allen Simpson had written the hit comedy TV show Steptoe and Son. This was the basis of what would become Sanford and Son in The States. Herman was a deal maker and through Ray had met Robert Stigwood of the Robert Stigwood Organization film empire. Through the Ray connection he was able to make a pitch to Robert Stigwood. Part of the negotiation was that R.S.O. Records would have the first choice of signing us. Robert consented and set things in motion. Go Herman.

This really raised the morale level. Along with the rehearsal monies, we each got a small living wage. I could pay my rent. I would go to the Robert Stigwood Organization offices at 67 Brook Street. There among his artists like the Bee Gees brothers and Eric Clapton, I would get some rent money for the measly flat that I had on McGregor Road, in Notting Hill Gate. I lived a few blocks from Island Records where I could stand in the street and hear Leslie West rehearse at concert volume through the thin walls.

Now it was time to seek a vocalist. We would be a three-piece band with a singer. We took out a Melody Maker ad and we got a call from Peter French, who had sung with Atomic Rooster and Leaf Hound. He had just returned from The States playing in the band Cactus, with Carmine Appice and Tim Bogert. Carmine and Tim had been one half of The Vanilla Fudge. They were disbanding that group to start a three-piece band with Jeff Beck, with no lead singer. Peter had it all, was a great guy and a full-on rocker looking for a good band to join. Initially he said he liked what he'd heard of our music but had to check out a band called March Hare that The Kinks were backing.

We thought that was his out and that there might be an age disparity, as we were all 21 years old and Peter was an older and more experienced 27. We were two Americans and a German. Peter is a proper Englishman. He came back the next day saying the other band wasn't right for him and told us he was keen on joining us. We rehearsed for a month at ACM Studios and then we were booked into C.B.S. Recording Studios in Tottenham Court Road, London. Top of the line. The big time. The recordings went well and we were offered a singles deal to get things started. We were very thrilled with that.

Then the bomb dropped. I was told by The Home Office of Immigration that my visa status was up and that I had to leave England. They had been looking for me for months but I had kept changing addresses. I filed some extensions, but it was to no avail. Even though I could speak American they wanted me to go home. At the same time the band Yes couldn't get a Greek keyboardist they wanted and the band Free couldn't get a Japanese bass player they wanted. I figured if the big guns couldn't get their guy, who was going to sponsor me? Herman had the same thing happen to him with immigration. He eventually returned to Germany and joined a new, unknown band called The Scorpions. The band carried on for a bit without me. Lee Jackson, bassist of The Nice, stepped in to replace me.

I had enjoyed my time and the people in England and learned more about the music business. I was never sure if I wanted to live there forever. As it turns out, I'm glad I came back. I said goodbye to driving on the wrong side of the road and great chocolate.

Have you ever felt you were a stranger in a strange land? Maybe you seemed a little out of place? So I stood in Boston's Logan Airport, an alien in my own country. I was back in the world of bib overalls, earth shoes and flannel shirts with my English clothes and stack-heeled blue boots. My mind was still thinking in terms of shillings, tuppences, and London Transport bus tickets. I needed a place to regroup and evaluate my next course of action.

I went back to my friends, Jack and Jim Weiner's place on Green Street in Brookline. Some roommates had come and gone, and some things had stayed the same. We were great friends and had much to talk about. They said I could stay there until I found my own place. That took a month because I knew where I didn't want to live, contrary to over a dozen jive real estate agents who tried to sell me on inferior places. Finally I found a quiet studio apartment for the right price in St. Mary's, on the Brookline Boston city line. The rear second floor apartment had sixteen-foot ceilings, a working 19th century fireplace, and huge bay windows overlooking The Wightman Mansion on Beech Mall. It was right on Beacon Street with a Green Line M.T.A. trolley right outside of my front door on the boulevard. It was a quick walk to Jack and Jim's. I would keep this apartment for the next 10 years, whether I was in New York or Los Angeles. I took the brass number 5 off the apartment door for good luck when I finally moved, and still have it inside my desk.

The networking resumed as I contacted my musical friends that I was back in town. Across Beacon St. from me was Babcock Park. It was a very nice small city park where I could spend time writing lyrics, poems, and thinking about musical ideas. One afternoon I went back to my apartment to get something to eat. I turned on my small black and white television and The Mike Douglas Show was on. It was a talk show that also had performances from comics and musical acts. In those days this show had a huge following.

Television on weekday afternoons was overrun with soap operas. Mike's show was a welcome addition.

From my kitchen, I could hear Mike Douglas hyping a great new band from England that was coming on to play. My curiosity brought me in to look at what he was talking about. There was this great new band in fine new suits with a limo outside and a big promotional campaign from their label, Chrysalis Records. Mike Douglas announced abys. Lo and behold, there was my mate, Michael Corby, with his dream band. Wow, it took a while for it all to register and I thought, good for him. The Babys would go on to great success. Unfortunately for Michael, the other three guys in the band didn't agree with some of his views and he was replaced. I saw Mike in Scotland recently, and we had some good laughs.

On my return to Boston I also learned that the local band Aerosmith had been signed to do their first album on Columbia Records. I thought to myself great for them. Hopefully, if they could do it, so could I. They were the one band from the area who I felt understood where I was coming from as we shared the same influences. The rock gods had looked down on them and they were off to a stellar career.

There were two Boston bands at the time that were like Three Dog Night. Both bands, Calamity Jane and Lovelace, featured three female vocalists. I was friends with Cindy Daley of Lovelace. One night we were at a late night musician's hangout, a Greek restaurant called the Aegean Faire in Kenmore Square. We talked about her band and how they were chasing a record contract. They were booked solid around the state and were going to record some demos. Cindy said she knew a band looking for a bass player. And I said "Really?" I asked, "How good are they?" She said they were an astounding band that mostly played their own music. I said, "What's their name?" She said Jack and I replied, "A band named Jack?" She said yes, but they had gone through a number of name changes. I asked "Like what?" She said a few more names that didn't ring any bells. Then I just about fell off my chair when she said that they had been called Fatback. "Fatback?!", I said incredulously, "Do they talk with Southern accents?" She said yes. I couldn't believe it. Fatback, recalling my friend Bill Buckland's outstanding review of them a few years earlier down in Connecticut. I said "Quick, give me the number". I will always be indebted to Cindy for getting us together.

    I called the number first thing in the morning and I got keyboard player Jimmy Waldo on the phone. He confirmed they were Fatback from Wilmington, North Carolina. He said they had changed singers and drummers and had also added a guitar player.

    They were looking to replace the original bass player, who they thought had a sound that was not heavy enough. I said "If you want bass, I've got it". Jimmy laughed and said to come out to audition on Saturday afternoon. He found my recent experience in London very interesting and told me they had auditioned sixteen bass players. This was a chance meeting that would span from the mid 70's until the present day.

Chapter 6

The band owned a house out in the suburbs in Medway Massachusetts. The split-level ranch was distinguished by a large box truck in the yard and numerous vehicles. I went down to the studio in the basement and couldn't believe the amount of gear they stuffed in there. Jimmy had keyboards that were modified and going through Marshall amps, plus the room was full of electronics. Guitarist John Fannon from Boston, Vocalist Kenny Melee from Long Island, New York, and drummer Hirsh Gardner from Toronto. Hirsh had just graduated from the Berklee College of Music.

I plugged in and thought it sounded great. Their original material was very professional. We were all the same age and had the same influences. This was the band I had been looking for far and wide. As well as having a Hammond B3 organ, Jimmy had electric pianos and a Mellotron like The Moody Blues. This gave the band a huge, orchestrated sound. Kenny had a fine voice and John played a great soaring melodic guitar over Hirsh`s pounding drums. In order to play college mixers, they had to play some cover songs. I said I was fine with that because the band was excellent. Jimmy said to call tomorrow at 5 PM and he would let me know who they chose. I said fine. The next day I called at 4 PM and said, "I'm the guy, right?" He said yes. Number seventeen was the winner. The vote was 3 to 1 in my favor.

In the 40 plus years we have played together, I`ve never found out who cast the nay vote.

It was January, and New Years Eve had come and gone. 1975 started off with Richard Nixon resigning from the presidency, the invention of The Rubik's Cube, the premiere of Saturday Night Live, and the beginning of Disco. I auditioned for the band, formerly known as Fatback, on January 17th. Within five rehearsals, we were off to play Bryant College, January 31st, in Smithfield, Rhode Island. We were recorded live on WJMF, the college radio station. It was the first time we (John, Jimmy, Hirsh and I) played live together. We were offered a copy of the concert, but I'm not sure if we ever received it.

We returned to Medway and rehearsed every day of the first two weeks in February. Then we played gigs in Keene State College, Keene, Vermont, The Rock Cliff in Stanstead, Quebec, Canada, Harvard University, and Concord Academy. The last week was booked for three nights at The Canteen in Lake George, New York followed by a gig at Plattsburgh State College in Plattsburgh, New York. That was followed by another week of gigs in Stanstead, Canada, and a Graham Junior College gig in Kenmore Square, less than a mile from my apartment– just over the Brookline city line.

I petitioned the band to use a new name. It really was a new band, although it had evolved from Fatback. Somewhere I got the idea of Target for a band name. There were no Target stores in Boston until 1999. I liked the idea that the name was one word and had a built-in logo, easy to read and remember. This was pre-Internet and we didn't know of any other bands called Target. It just so happened that Jimmy Jamison, future singer of Survivor, had a group in Nashville, Tennessee of the same name and was signed to a record deal. We didn't use the name long enough to see any repercussions from any other band using the name Target around the country.

We continued playing weekly around the Northern New England, Quebec circuit. We were booked by the Ed Malhoit Agency in Claremont, New Hampshire. Ed kept us busy, but eventually we felt that we couldn't go any further in the club scene. We wanted to stop playing cover songs and devote our time to writing original music and securing a record contract. John previously had managers named Neil and Lloyd Grossman. He felt if he could reconnect with them, they might possibly manage us. I read in the Boston Phoenix that they were managing a Linda Ronstadt type artist named Annie McLoone and that she was going to be recording for RCA in the late fall.

As the summer was winding down, we were playing for a week at Bourbon Street in Newport, Rhode Island. John and Jimmy asked me to take a walk out on the beach with them. They explained that Neil and Lloyd didn't want to manage the band but had offered both of them to join Annie's band. They said they were going to do it. Good for them, not so good for me. These are my guys seven years before we broke up the band New England. The best laid plans of mice and men.

I took the frame of mind that although their decision to leave the band for a better opportunity was not in my best interest, they had every right to move on. It was better to remain friends and possibly reunite down the road. Better not to burn bridges in friendship or business. If I had the offer, would I go? Probably, perhaps possibly. We'll never know.

Target played our final bookings at The Chopping Block in Ludlow, Vermont and The 19th Green in Rutland, Vermont. We were one of the last bands to play at The Groggery in Boston. The Groggery rocked. It always had a line going around the block. John had a job there at one point flipping hamburgers when he was in the group Flash Puddin. Target's last gig was in Rutland, Vermont at Gigi`s. The manager was a complete jerk. We left our one roadie behind with a 26 foot rental truck. He wasn't moving fast enough for the manager, who pushed him down and started throwing our gear into the parking lot. The manager then drove off. The club had a huge 20 foot by 20 foot plate glass window in the front of the club. Somehow, on the way out, our truck mysteriously went into reverse and took out the whole front window and then proceeded to drive off into the night towards Boston. Target went out with a bang.

Chapter 7

Just after Target disbanded, we recorded at Intermedia Studios on Newbury Street in Boston. We were minus Kenny Melee who wanted to pursue singing Disco. John had elected to sing lead vocals on a few new songs he had written. One of them, "Familiar Faces" was released on our 5 CD New England Archives album. John was stuck for the lyric for the verse, "Was it Leeds or …Too? He asked me what English city might fit? I said how about Wembley? It was a keeper. The song titled "Green Paper Doll" was about money. Unfortunately, we lost our original cassette copies of it. It was interesting being a 4 piece band and it was the way of the future. We would have to wait for the Annie McLoone record to come and go and I would have to return from Los Angeles for us to write a new chapter in the meta evolution of Fatback.

I saw The Annie McLoone Band play at Jack`s in Cambridge. After they finished recording their record at Long View Farm Studios in North Brookfield, Massachusetts, they were going on tour supporting Pure Prairie League. The band was a bit mismatched. They had a jazz drummer from the Berklee College of music, a classical bassist from Boston University, and Annie, who was a bit of a hell raiser. Throw in two rock guys and fire up the station wagon for a winter tour. There would be no second album.

A friend of mine, Jonathan Herndon, had a brother who owned a warehouse in Cambridge. It was a precursor to Whole Foods, and they stocked large quantities of rice and grains. Jonathan let my friends and I jam there at night. I invited my music friends to come over and play for our own amusement. My good friend Larry Dalton played drums for most of the jams. A young fiery guitarist who played like Ritchie Blackmore came in one weekend from Washington, D.C. Great guitar player. A few months later I gave Hal a few phone numbers when he went off to London like I had done earlier. Years later when we were searching for a replacement for Steve Vai, I thought about him and called his mother. It was always good in those days to keep friends' parents' phone numbers, as they were more stationary. His mom said he had joined a band in England and I asked if she knew the name. I was stunned when she said Dire Straits. I went out to a record store to find the Dire Straits albums and sure thing, my friend Hal Lindes was in Dire Straits. Very cool.

I met a Hammond B3 organist named Holly and her friend, Dan, who played drums. They wanted to do progressive rock like Emerson Lake and Palmer. Each time a song ended the drummer would jump up and click his sticks in triumph. That was very unusual to say the least. About five years later, Holly Knight was also being managed like myself, by Bill Aucoin in New York City. Her band Spider included Anton Fig, future David Letterman Band drummer. Since then, Holly has been inducted into The Songwriters Hall of Fame and won thirteen ASCAP Awards for writing hit songs such as The Warrior and Love Is A Battlefield for Pat Benatar. We are good friends and laugh at what a small world it is, remembering our time in Cambridge at the warehouse in Central Square.

As the year came to an end I spoke to my friend Greg Chansky. He had written a new set of songs since we had moved back to Boston. He was going to Triple AAA Studios in Boston to record them and asked me if I would like to play bass on them. I said sure. There were four songs. I liked them all. One of them, Circular Motion, I thought was a hit for sure. Greg had his brother, Paul, on keyboards and Howie Greenberg, who had played drums on the Boston demo that was circulating around at the time. Greg also talked his friends Steven Tyler from Aerosmith and Billy Squire of The Sidewinders to sing background vocals.

Our friends, Barry Brandt, Mickie Jones, and Frank Domino had formed a new group named Angel in Washington DC. with Greg Giuffria and Punky Meadows. The band signed to Casablanca Records, relocating to Los Angeles. They received an incredible financial investment for the times. Angel was being talked about as the white KISS by Neil Bogart, who had signed both bands to his new record label.

Their manager, David Joseph, heard Greg's demo through the guys in Angel and offered to bring him to Los Angeles for management. Greg said he couldn't promise anything to me, but if I came to Los Angeles maybe there would be a gig for me. Greg gave me a cassette demo and Tom Schultz's phone number, saying that his up-and-coming band called Boston had just signed to Epic Records and needed a bass player. I liked the music, but I liked the music of Target and Greg's music more. I never made that phone call and to this day I don't regret it a bit. I kept the cassette Greg gave me though.

Chapter 8

I was moving to the land of dreams, where careers were created or crushed. The City of Legends and the home of galactic star power. A place where snow only existed up in the mountains. I was moving to Hollywood, California.

Westward Ho! And so began the music business migration to Los Angeles. 1976 It was the 200th Anniversary of America. The Bicentennial was happening, and the country was in a good mood. Everyone I knew on the East Coast would eventually go to Los Angeles to pursue their music careers. There was a shift from the established music capitals like New York City, London, and Nashville, seeking the more pleasant weather and lifestyle of Southern California. The West Coast recording studios were enjoying a booming business, and more music business personnel were electing to move there. Even Motown Records, the champions of Detroit, had pulled up its roots and moved it all to 6255 Sunset Boulevard in 1972.

Unlike my move to London, I elected to keep my apartment in Brookline. As it turned out, it was a smart thing to do. I had friends that did business in Boston, and in the pre Air BnB days, they could pay my rent and save money on hotels. I left everything intact. My great friend, Charlie Earley, and my brother, Peter, were driving out to visit friends in Arizona. They would drive me out to Los Angeles and then continue on their trip. I had the smallest U-haul trailer that could carry my trusty Ampeg SVT amplifier with two 8/X10 speaker cabinets in leather strapped custom trap cases. I had hitchhiked to

California previously, and this was a time to enjoy the ride following the western sunset. Once again, I was going into the great unknown sight unseen.

Greg had found a nice guest house apartment in the Hancock Park area of Hollywood, which is where many movie stars lived prior to the homes being built in Beverly Hills. The chaos was instantaneous; nothing had changed as Greg struggled to bounce the complexity of life with the challenge of playing music. He had a great rehearsal hall— the former Columbia Pictures Studios lot at Sunset Boulevard. Gower had been turned into a music complex owned by Studio Instrument Rentals. There were a dozen soundstages that had seen the likes of The Three Stooges and dozens of others who had filmed there in the 30s. Each soundstage was a small theater with a stage and a few dozen rows of seats. When I went there, they were occupied by Deep Purple, Frank Zappa, Cher, America, and Donovan, to name a few. A mecca of music activity. While the bands rehearsed side by side, the music business-people were in a flurry on the lot. A great place to network.

The great bass player Jaco Pastorious had just released his solo album that set the bass playing world on its ear with his amazing technique. Greg, more than anyone else I knew, truly flipped-out and decided that he had to have a bass player that played in this new, jazzy, funky style. I'll be the first to admit that ain't me. This added to Greg's frustrations, and it continues to this day in his endless search for new musicians. I knew that although we were, and still remain good friends, I was not destined for Greg's creativity.

I was new in town and getting used to seeing people like Dick Van Dyke at the gas station pumping his own gas. It was time to branch out and seek new opportunities in Los Angeles. Other than my East Coast friends I had a hard time finding a local heavy rock band to join that played the music I heard in my heart. Most of the music was more laid back, and in a more acoustic guitar vein like Poco or The Eagles. At The Starwood I watched Quiet Riot. They were doing very well for themselves with Randy Rhodes on guitar. Van Halen had yet to be discovered and sign a record deal. It was very frustrating trying to find the kind of music I had made with Target in the land of the sun, surf, and beach boys. I saw my good friend Ted McKenna play at The Starwood. He had left the Alex Harvey band and was on tour playing drums with the great Rory Gallagher.

A few of my friends from the band Angel and I went to lunch one day at the trendy Hamburger Hamlet in Century City. It was located on Century Park East among the towers of movie and music business offices and was a great place for lunch. We were sitting in the lobby waiting for a table and someone sat down next to me. I was mildly surprised that it was Sally Struthers from the television show, All In The Family. We sat and watched the parade of people go by. An attractive blonde woman in a white business suit, carrying a briefcase, came up to me. She told me I looked interesting to her and introduced herself as the editor of Playgirl Magazine. My friends couldn't believe it. Neither could I. She said she would like to put me in the magazine and explained the different payments for the three features. The full spread would pay the rent for a long time. To say I wasn't flattered wouldn't be true. The best part was that my friends' egos were on the floor. She gave me her card telling me to send in some nude photos of myself and that selection was done by a panel of Playgirl Magazine executives. In the world of today's mores I would be considered a hero, but back then the world was much more conservative. I didn't want to jeopardize any future musical situations, and most of all I didn't want my mother to endure any repercussions. I thought about it for a week and decided to decline the offer. I still have the white embossed business card she gave me.

I reunited with my friends, Jon Hyde and Michael Monarch. They were on top of the world. Their new band Detective was being backed by Led Zeppelin's Jimmy Page on Swan Song Records. Jon said my frustration in finding musicians was the same reason they had gone to London to find bandmates. I went with Jon one day as he bought two brand new Gibson J-200 acoustic guitars. A six string, and the other a twelve string, with his record advance money. They were gearing up for gigs with KISS and would play Madison Square Garden. I saw my friends from Angel play at The Santa Monica Civic Center. Little did I know that in three years' time, New England would get encores at Madison Square Garden and sell out The Santa Monica Civic Center. After the concert, Angel drove off in two limousines to begin their first North American tour. They should have leased a tour bus, as both limos overheated in the hot desert of Arizona.

Larry Dalton's wife, Anne, suggested I look up her friend Cheryl Leitch, who worked for BMI. Her roommate, Jan Turling, worked for Songwriter Magazine. They shared a three-bedroom bungalow off Sunset near Ralph's Supermarket in Hollywood. A third roommate, Michael, was on the road working for Little Feat. Cheryl said I could stay there with them. Through her I met the guys in Legs Diamond who were doing well. There was an old funky Volvo parked in the backyard. One day Cheryl asked me if I would help her friend move his car out to the street to jump the battery. I said sure. It was Jackson Brown. I started playing with another friend of theirs named Peter Jacob who was a guitarist. We played together with a drummer named Jack White, working on some songs Peter had written.

An opportunity came along for us to audition for Al Stewart before The Year of The Cat was released. I knew of him from living in London, but he had not yet broken in The States. He was looking for a local band that was tight to back him up on his next tour. I learned the music of his previous album and the music from the unreleased Year Of The Cat. It went well. Al's manager, J.P., knew my former booking agent friend Ken Griffin from Connecticut. He gave me a big bear hug and told me I had the gig and that Al liked my bass playing. The tour would pay $1000 a week, which was big money in those days. I was pinching myself that this would transpire.

    Then the phone rang. It was Jimmy Waldo. He said the Annie Mcloone Band had parted ways and that he, John, and Hirsh had got back together again to work on original music. He said they couldn't find anyone who played like me in Boston. Would I come back? I said no, telling them I thought I had the Al Stewart gig with a 90% chance at going on the tour. Also, these were the guys that had defected to the Annie Mcloone Band leaving me high and dry. He called a week later and asked again. I said no, saying it was sunny and 80 degrees in L.A, and probably snowing in Boston. He called a third time, and I finally said yes. I thought it was better to be 25% of my own band than to be a side man who can get fired at any given moment on a fixed salary. I also believed in the music so much that I was willing to risk a second chance.

Chapter 9

I thanked Cheryl and Jan for their hospitality and good times as I bought a one-way plane ticket to Boston. I shipped my amplifier and speaker cabinets on air freight. When it arrived in Boston I was mysteriously never charged for the bill. The three pieces weighed in at slightly less than 400 lbs. I took a cab to Brookline, turned my key, and I was home again after a six month journey. Everything was as I had left it. What a great feeling to be back in my comfortable flat. The Music Gods were winking at me.

Jimmy's biggest selling point of why I should come back to Boston at the end of 1976 was that John had a connection to a recording studio and we were being offered free recording time. John had talked to the owner of Earmark Studios in Philadelphia. Steve Bruno was a friend of John's by way of another friend's introduction. He had an up-to-date sixteen track recording studio and was very successful recording the R&B bands of the Philly sound. He was anxious to record with a rock group that would be creative and inventive in the studio, much like The Beatles and Queen. We made an agreement that if we ever got a major record deal, it would be done at Earmark, or we would pay for the studio time used at a reduced rate. We thought that was a fair deal and it eventually worked out for all of us in spades. It was well worth it. It was unheard of for most unknown bands to have sixteen track demos at the time.

Prior to John getting married he rented a 19th century house with two of his best friends. The house sat on a seventeen-acre lot in the suburban woods of Braintree

Massachusetts. It had a built-in pool, and a small cottage that the owner had once used for an office. Hirsh and his friends took over the rent and the small cottage was remodeled into a rehearsal studio. The inner walls were removed, leaving a large room and a small room. Hirsh single handedly took out the chimney and the bathroom with a claw hammer. The small room was rented out to local bands at night to pay our electricity bill. If The Band had Music from Big Pink we had Music from Great White.

This would become the home base of the reworked Fatback/Target. It was far enough into the woods that the cottage could not be seen or heard. We began a routine of non-stop rehearsing and reworking John's songs. By this time, Jimmy had sold the Medway house and I got him an apartment in my building in Brookline. We would take the trolley to Park Street station and switch for the train to Braintree, where John would pick us up. We rehearsed every weekday, 11am to 4pm. for the next few years. We would reverse the trolley ride to get home. I carried my bass in its original black Tolex case on the train before gig bags became popular. Through the hordes of commuters, we made our way.

We did a series of three road trips to Earmark Studios in Philadelphia. It was a 6 hour drive from Boston and we would stay in motels in New Jersey, on the other side of the Ben Franklin Bridge to save money. It truly was remarkable that we got to use a top of the line sixteen track studio to record the songs we put together. The studio was beautiful inside and had all of the state-of-the-art recording equipment we needed.

We began with the songs "Candy" and "It's So Easy." working our way up a year later to "Don't Ever Wanna Lose Ya". Each time we would drive home from recording in Philadelphia, John and I would play a cassette of the new tracks over and over. We celebrated our good fortune in a smoky haze. Each set of songs made us believe in ourselves more and more. We were on the right track to join the major leagues.

Steve Bruno helped us in many ways. He got us a musician from the Philadelphia Orchestra, who was leaving a session, to play glockenspiel on the outro of the song "Nothing To Fear". He also helped us to try and procure a manager. He knew Grover Washington Jr's manager, Lloyd Remick. Grover Washington Jr is known as the father of smooth jazz and for his dreamy saxophone work. Lloyd was very interested in hearing us play live in a showcase situation. We had a meeting and agreed to a time and place.

We booked Studio Instrument Rentals in Manhattan and chose one of the larger rooms. This meant tearing everything apart in Braintree and driving the truckload of gear to New York City. Even though we hadn't played live in a while, we were in great shape. Rehearsing everyday keeps you sharp. Steve and Lloyd Remick arrived, and we began our set. Halfway in we blew the power to the room and it turned into bedlam. The staff claimed no one had ever blown out the power, not even The Rolling Stones. We said that may be true, but we're on the clock, so please get it fixed ASAP. We lost our momentum. This was a big deal for us. We swore never again would we do showcases for business-people without being in full control. From now on, all showcases were done in Braintree and we had great success. We felt Lloyd was probably not suited for us, noting that he had no other rock bands on his roster. We were building momentum.

Earmark Studios was located just up the street from the Philadelphia Museum of Art. It's where Sylvester Stallone filmed the famous scene of Rocky Balboa running up the large staircase in triumph. Each time we recorded at Steve's studio, the four of us would run up the steps of the museum yelling and screaming that we would be victorious. It's good for the body to scream out now and again. Each time we got a new set of 16 track songs, we got closer and closer to major interest in us.

Jimmy needed to drive down to Redding, Connecticut to have his Mellotron worked on. We played our latest demo for the owner and he loved it. He said his friend would really like to hear It. Would we mind if he came over for a listen? We said sure. A few minutes later a brand new black Mercedes showed up and out stepped Dick Wagner. Dick was the lead guitarist in The Frost from Detroit. He had played on Alice Cooper and Aerosmith album sessions just to name a few. We got in the car and Dick loved the music on the tape we played for him. He asked if we had a producer yet and we replied that we were looking. Dick said he would like to come to Boston the next weekend and work with us for a day to show what he could do. We agreed.

Dick showed up with a trunk full of B.C. Rich guitars and we plugged him into a Marshall half stack amp. We started playing and I looked at the five of us and I thought how cool this was. Dick began to make arrangement changes and we thought we were losing the essence of our sound. We didn't want to sound like anybody else. We told Dick we loved what he did but we weren't ready to decide yet on a producer. It was a great shot in the arm to have someone so successful spend time with us and give us a big dose of encouragement. Our confidence rose higher knowing that we were on the right road. I might not have had a car, but I was speeding down that highway of dreams and not looking back.

Chapter 10

Trust: "Reliance on the integrity, strength and ability of a person or a thing". Is there a situation or person that you believed would do right by you? Someone that would be truthful, and have your best interests in mind at all times? We were coming into a new phase where we began building a team that would promote us around the world. We would now have to put our trust in others. There are no great bands without great managers.

Managers fall into what I call the David and Goliath Theory. You can have your cousin or best friend devote himself to the cause, willing to lay his life down for you in rush hour traffic. He may have all the good intentions in the world but has no connections. The other side of that is having Mr. Big be your manager. A mover and a shaker who can make one phone call and instill fear among people from coast to coast, around the world. The downside of a manager like that is that they have major clients who demand their time. You're not the most important horse in his stable. Management has to have good faith in their artist to fight the battles in the show biz arena. The choice of the two is yours, and it's like walking blindly over hot coals. Everyone must be prepared for the flare ups.

During the first two years in Braintree, we had no need for a manager. All of our effort went into the music and recording in Philadelphia. We only gave out a few recordings to people who we thought could help us. I had a friend named Paul Mcalpine who was a very creative photographer and who had taken photos of Target. He shot all the rock concerts in Boston and knew many of the record company reps. We had fun driving around the city in Paul's Mustang taking interesting photos. I had given him a copy of our demo. Paul knew Kurt Nerlinger, who was Elektra Records' Northeastern rep. He had helped break Queen in America and was instrumental in getting The Cars their record deal. He was Elektra Records' promotion man of the year in 1978. Paul played him our demo and he really liked what he heard. He asked, would it be possible to come to a rehearsal in Braintree? We said yes.

Kurt came down to rehearsal from his home in Manchester By The Sea in his BMW 320i and wearing driving gloves. We played live for him. He couldn't get over how much we sounded like our recordings and even heavier live. Each week his Elektra Records job took him past our studio. He had to drive down to Providence, Rhode to meet with FM radio program directors and retail record stores. Each time he came by he brought a six pack of beer and free copies of recently released records. He was excited because his record company promotion friend Charlie McKenzie had quit his job to manage the band Boston and did quite well for himself.

It wasn't long before Kurt popped the question of him becoming our manager. I asked him if he'd ever booked a band into a Knights of Columbus hall or a Grange hall. He said no. I asked, How can you get us into Madison Square Garden?" We were concerned about that. The one thing he did was suggest a name which we hadn't thought of yet. We called ourselves Fannon for a bit, but everyone said Fanny or Phantom and we knew that wouldn't work. He suggested the name New England and we thought about it. John and I were from New England and the name described the new English style of music we were playing. We thought if anyone had the audacity or the balls to use that name after Boston's success, we were that band. Bring on the heat. We were ready. We were not the conspiracy theory that a major manager and record company put us together to emulate Boston. We had been around and were the real deal.

Kurt asked if it was okay to send our tape to Queen's guitarist Brian May. We were interested to see if he might produce the band. The answer came back that he liked the music and was interested, depending upon his schedule. Then something really momentous occurred: Kurt played our tape for his friend, Ric Ailberte, at a KISS gig in Providence. Ric had also worked promotion with Elektra and was now in charge of promotion for the KISS Organization in New York City. He loved the music and asked if he could come the next day and see us live. Kurt said the band was amazing and that we were nice guys. We got a late night phone call. Would we play live for Ric the following day on short notice? Everything was set up in our studio just how we wanted, and we said yes. Gene Simmons called Rick in the morning at his hotel and said, "New England, I like that name."

In our isolation we would have friends drop by occasionally. We would use them as a sounding board at the end of rehearsal to play songs for them and get their reaction. Of course they were favorable but it helped us keep our fingers on playing live. We played the short set and Ric was impressed. Kurt was smiling too. Here was a great band in the woods that was ready for prime time. Ric said he was going to call KISS's manager, Bill Aucoin, in New York and tell him of their discovery.

The train was leaving the station on the long track to musical recognition. We were ready to compete with all of the other bands on the scene and take no prisoners. In the midst of our exuberance, the Snake would soon raise its head.

Chapter 11

And so it began, the line of black limos coming from Los Angeles, New York, and London from Boston's Logan Airport, driving into the woods of Braintree in secrecy. We had always kept a low profile and didn't advertise who we were showcasing for. We had our rehearsal studio tweaked-out for maximum sound performance. Loud but not too loud. If we had to move it, the gear would never work right. We were playing on our terms and we sounded awesome in that little wooden house..

First and foremost was Bill Aucoin, the man behind KISS. Bill had managed Piper with Billy Squire and Starz. He also managed Toby Beau who, at the time, had the current Number One hit with "My Angel Baby." He was soft-spoken and extremely knowledgeable. We played for Bill, with Rick and Kurt in attendance. We played two short sets with an intermission of a fine spread of cokes, crackers, and cheese from across the street from Kmart. Bill was relaxed and took the tension out of what we were about to do.

No pressure, as Bill sat on a folding chair ten feet from my bass amp. We were giving it our best performance, pretending we were playing in an arena with full lights and sound. Three songs into the set a very large blue electric flash shot out of the back of my amplifier. I immediately hit the standby switch and we took a time out. Everyone went into panic mode except Bill and I. He was unfazed and cool as a cucumber. I looked at my amp and said to it that I had cared for it from coast to coast, with its custom cases and coddling and I'd be damned if it was going to let me down at this moment. After a short break I turned it back on and we resumed our showcase, finishing all of the songs. Bill really liked what he heard and saw. We made plans to travel down to New York City to see what he could do for us. The next day we came to rehearsal. I flipped the amp on and it blew 100%. I was OK with it though, as it had held the line.

Arrangements were made for ourselves and Kurt to fly from Boston to New York City. We were met by a limousine and brought to Bill's office at 645 Madison Avenue. The KISS headquarters was a flurry of activity on two floors. They had their own production department, promotion department, and legal team under one roof. They also had an office in Los Angeles on Wilshire Boulevard in the Tishman Building.

It just so happened that Bill's apartment was on the cover of Architectural Digest that month. He lived on the 37th floor of the Olympic Towers with neighbors like Jackie Kennedy Onassis. We were wined and dined like royalty and Bill explained what he saw for us and how he could help us achieve all of our objectives. We met the super efficient Stephanie Tudor, Bill's assistant. Ric's assistant, and supergirl of promotion, Gail Rogers who had previously worked for Alice Cooper. Kenny Anderson in production was the man behind all things guitars, lights, staging, and touring.

If there was a Goliath manager, it was Bill Aucoin. It took us a few days back home to process the whirlwind we had just seen up close. The next step was for Kurt to go to New York City to see what kind of deal he could broker for himself with Aucoin Management / Rock Steady Productions. Before he left, he came by with a document called 'a letter of intent'. It specified that we would enter a formal management contract with Kurt as leverage in his meeting. We had always said Kurt could be our road manager or liaison but never our manager due to his lack of experience.

The letter was a binding legal document and Kurt swore he would tear it up on his return. We took a chance that he would honor his word. He went down to see Aucoin Management and they offered him 5% of the band's gross. Not a bad deal if things go well. He said it was not good enough on his return home and stormed off in this BMW 320i with our letter of intent fully intact. The Snake was about to strike out at all of us.

Prior to meeting Bill Aucoin, John had reached the office of Clive Davis at Arista Records. Clive actually returned a phone call and we all stood around by the house phone as his assistant said, "Hold for Clive." It goes without saying that Clive Davis is an icon unto himself in the music business. He is responsible for establishing the careers of more than a dozen famous artists. When we got Bill involved, the stakes went up and we created a buzz that sent record company presidents and vice presidents to our door. This is a list of who's who:

Number One. Arista Records president Clive Davis and his assistant, Bob Fidden, came from New York City and heard us. Clive sat in the same folding chair in front of my amp that Bill had used. It was a pinch me moment. Clive said he had just signed the Kinks, one of my favorite bands, but they were pop and he wanted a heavy sound like we had.

Number Two. Danny Goldberg, Vice President of Elektra Records Los Angeles, and producer Chuck Plotkin, who had just finished producing a Bruce Springsteen album. Chuck talked about emotional architecture and arrangement tonalities to us. We loved that conversation. The game had gone to hardball. They had just signed The Cars from Boston and wanted us as the American Queen.

Number Three. Chrysalis Records. President Chris Wright flew in from London. They had many of the bands we loved. Chris told me afterwards as we walked across the lawn that we were the best band he had seen since he had signed Procol Harum to Chrysalis.

Number Four. R.S.O. Records London. Al Coury, ex-president of Capitol Records, Vice President and co-founder of the Robert Stigwood Organization. They were coming off the bestselling record of all time with Saturday Night Fever. Al took us to dinner in his hometown of Worcester, Massachusetts. Money was no object.

Number Five .Epic Records. New York City. President Lenny Petze, former member of the Rondells. Lenny and his New England promo rep, Lenny Collins, were local guys and considered us the local team, off to play the Yankees. They were great guys, boulders among stones.

Number Six. Infinity / MCA. New York City. Ron Alexenbourg, former president of Epic Records, was starting a new label funded by M.C.A. Records. They had a small roster of bands and a handpicked national promotion staff from all of the other labels. They had a large budget to work with.

Some of the labels we felt were better for solo artists rather than rock bands or had poor distribution. If a record became a big hit some labels had a distribution problem of getting lots of records to the stores in time. With major labels it's easy to fall through the cracks with a multitude of famous label mates releasing their records at the same time. We chose Ron Alexembourg, thinking that with a small roster they would have to work very hard to promote us and money was not a problem. We could choose wherever we wanted to record, in any studio in the world.

We resumed rehearsals, working on new songs, when there was a loud knock on the door. We had boarded up the windows and couldn't see outside. A U.S. Marshal stepped inside and gave each one of us a subpoena with our names on it. We were being sued by Kurt Nerlinger, wait for it, for $1,000,000.00 each. He was also suing Bill Aucoin and MCA records each for a million dollars in U.S. Federal Court in New York City. The Snake had come out of the grass and showed his true colors. Everyone was dumbfounded and very angry. Could all of our hard work be for nothing? The best laid plans of mice and men. Mr. Nerlinger had his little letter of intent and cited all the time he had spent with us and had a list of phony investments and expenditures that he made up.

Amazing to us was that Bill Aucoin and M.C.A. were going to go to battle for us and not drop us like a hot potato. Regardless, it was going to cost us a pretty penny to hire a major league entertainment lawyer to represent us in the State of New York. We retained Martin Silfen, who represented Billy Joel and other luminaries. He was a Fulbright scholar and also taught entertainment law at New York University, in New York City. Kurt chose Peter Parcher, another high-powered New York City entertainment lawyer.

Both sides went head-to-head, resulting in a settlement of us having to pay $30,000.00 to Nerlinger because of that damn little piece of paper. We gave him an initial payment of $3000.00 and never paid another cent, nor again heard from our "friend". The Snake silently slithered into the grass and away from the record business, never to be seen again. We were christened into the world of major league music lawsuits. A wiseman once said, "Never trust a man wearing driving gloves and bearing gifts."

Gallery

Eric

ELEASE   CONTACT: IDA S. LANGSAM

Rock and roll sports seems to be a recurring trend. British rockers like Elton John, Rod Stewart and Mick Jagger favor soccer; American stars Styx frequently attend hockey matches; and piano man Billy Joel has sung the praises of baseball's New York Yankees. Now comes supergroup KISS showing an affinity for -- softball!

The demons of rock proved to be demons on the ball field as well when they and their financial advisors, Glickman/Marks Management, challenged the band's management company, Aucoin, to a Saturday game in New York's Central Park. Gene Simmons, Paul Stanley and Eric Carr of KISS played for the Glickman/Marks Cheaters, with Ace Frehley slugging for the Aucoin All Stars, along with Jimmy Waldo and Gary Shea of New England, and Amanda Blue, Keith Lentin and Anton Fig of Spider.

The final score was 18 to 12 in favor of the All Stars, despite exceptional playing by Gene and Eric, and Paul's being voted the afternoon's Most Valuable Player. We're sure the rematch will be played with a vengeance.

Circus magazine top 4 new bands of 1979: 1 The Knack, 2 The Cars, 3 New England, 4 Molly Hatchell

Gary Shea and Steve Vai

Alcatrazz l to 4, Steve Vai, Graham Bonnet, Jan Uvena,
Jimmy Waldo, Gary Shea

Alcatrazz, l to r, Jimmy Waldo, Yngwie Malmsteen, Graham Vonnet, Jan Uvena, Gary Shea

Larry Paterson, Gary Shea, Doogie White, Joe Stump

Herman Rarebell Peter French, Gary Shea

Gary Shea, James Brown

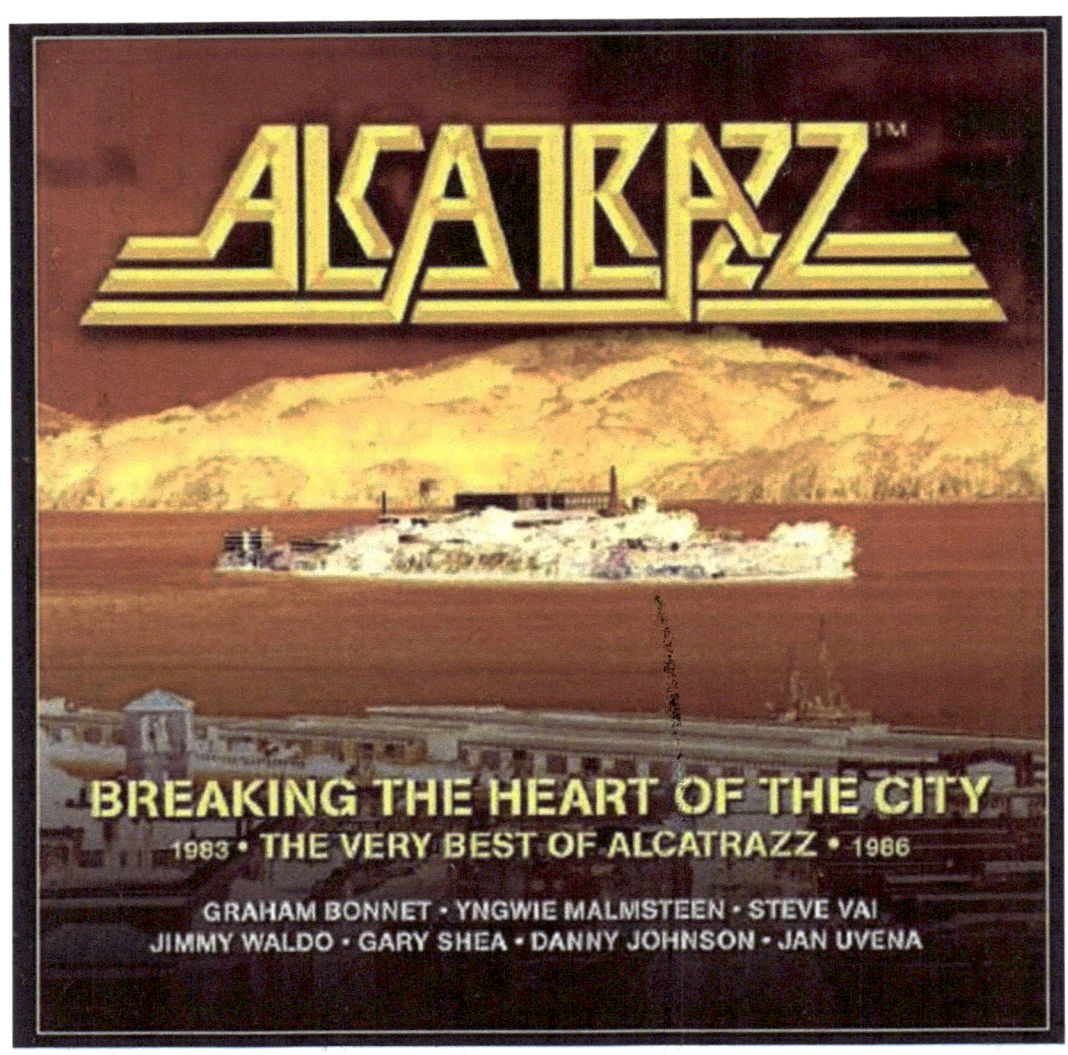

Alcatrazz Larry Paterson, Jimmy Waldo, Joe Stump, Gary Shea, Doogie White

Liberty Street, Southington Connecticut

John Hyde, Michael Monarch

Davlen Studios seated Producer Paul Stanley, Ron Alexenburg President of Infinity Records, standing - John Fannon, Bud O'Shea Infinity Records VP, Hirsh Gardner, Al Bergamo President MCA Distributing, engineer Mike Stone, Gary Shea, Jimmy Waldo

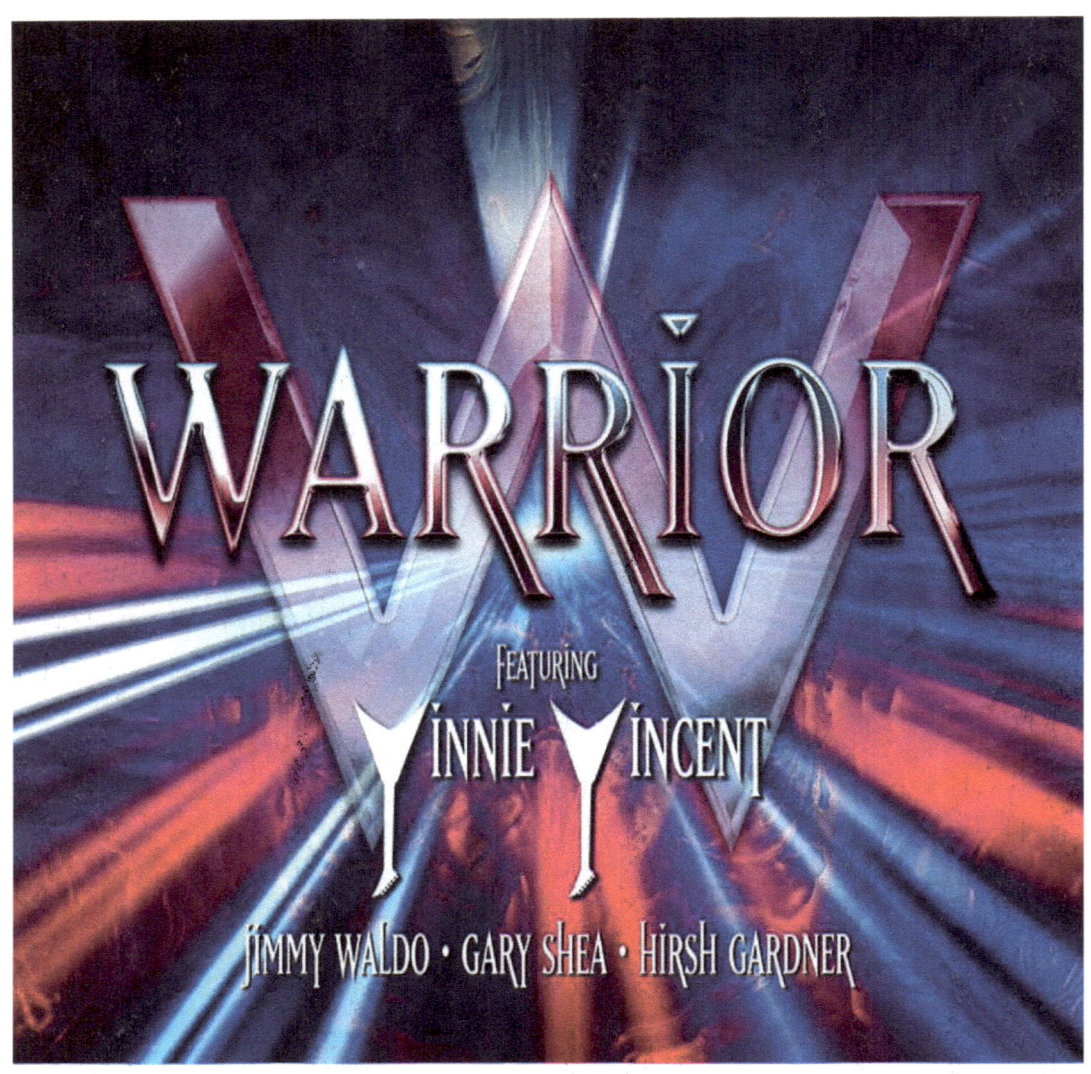

Chapter 12

With the Nerlinger mess finished it was now time to negotiate our management contract with Bill Aucoin and our recording contract with Infinity Records. We chose Marty Silfen in New York City to interpret our management contract and Zalkind and Zalkind in Boston to review our lengthy record deal. Lawyers have a great way of continuous job security by writing everything in a language that only they and others like them can understand. You pay them for their interpretation and it's not cheap.

The first order of business was what to do about Steve Bruno and our Earmark Studios demo recording. We were advised that since we hadn't signed a contract, nothing prevented us from walking away and not paying. We knew we were going to re-record all of our songs to 24 track and it wasn't going to be in Philadelphia. Steve had put many hours of time into our music and had missed family matters that his wife was not happy about. Steve asked for $28,000 in studio time, a fair price for the time spent over a year and a half.

We discussed among ourselves what was best to do and we unanimously chose to pay the full price of $28,000. Divided by four, it was $7000 apiece. In 1978 that was more than enough to buy a brand new Chevrolet Camaro Z-28 or a comparable Ford Mustang. I hadn't owned a car for ten years and I decided Steve was our friend and I continued taking the subway. The band felt that without Steve, we wouldn't be in the great position we were in.

Contracts are about only one thing, money; how much and for how long. Arguing over a half cent royalty may seem petty but over the course of a long career it can accumulate into thousands of dollars for the artist. Successful artists get royalty checks each quarter of the year, referred to as mailbox money. They come in the mail from earnings from record sales, film soundtracks, and even plays in the jukeboxes around the world. When we initially signed with Bill, he took 25% of our gross monies. Compared to Colonel Tom Parker's 50% of Elvis that's not so bad. He said when it was time, he would drop down to 20% so that we could hire a business manager.

In time that's what Bill did, and we hired Bert Padell, the business manager to the stars at 1775 Broadway in Times Square. He had dozens of A List celebrity clients who gave him 5 % of their gross income to manage their business affairs for them. Bert could have his team buy you a ranch in Wyoming, do all of the paperwork, and give you the keys while you attended to matters elsewhere.

For us though, having one of Bert's staff take a check for deposit a few blocks away and then get billed for it made no sense. If we got a check from the label, we not only paid Bert's 5%, but we incurred office fees of hundreds of dollars for an office employee to deposit the check across town at a bank. There were other fees as well, such as going to the post office. We eventually moved all our financial business to Boston and wished Bert well. We became New England Productions. I could go downtown to our post office box and pick up a check and deposit it for a round trip fare on the subway of less than two dollars. We then hired a local tax accountant to advise us, rounding out our new business structure.

In a management contract, there are pitfalls to look for. For instance, if you buy your mom a Hallmark store franchise, does your manager get a percentage of that or just your musical work? There are many parts to consider. New England, as we were now known, bought out two small bands using the name so that we could clear the trademark issues. We hired Zalkind and Zalkind in Boston to negotiate our record deal with Infinity Records. We wanted our main lawyers to be in Boston for easy access. Zalkind and Zalkind did a good job with our Infinity deal. We noticed though that there were many calls which talked about the Red Sox more than our business, plus there were conference calls with multiple lawyers charging $350 an hour. It turned out we were billed $12,000 over what we had run up. We protested the bill which was then readjusted and we parted ways.

Now was the time to pick a producer for our first album. Being a new band, no one would let us do our own producing. We had thought of possibly getting Gus Dudgeon, of Elton John fame, who was a great arranger. There was also Roy Thomas Baker from Queen, but he was booked and we could not wait around. Fortunately, Brian May of Queen had received our demo and liked it. He had a schedule conflict, but he had driven our demo over to Roy Thomas Baker's understudy, Mike Stone, and put it in his mailbox to listen to.

Back in New York an option arose that we were surprised about. Mike Stone was working on some KISS music. Bill asked if we would consider Paul Stanley and Mike Stone as producers? It was a unique opportunity. Paul was very qualified and would make a fine coach. Mike was the recording console genius of the big sound. He was also already familiar with our music. It also wouldn't hurt if some of the KISS Army fans happened to like us too.

We decided to record the new album at Davlen Studios Los Angeles, the vocals at Electric Ladyland Studios in New York City, and the mixing would be done at Trident Studios in London. Mike would fly over some extra gear and his own playback monitors.

Mike and Paul became the next guests of ours in Braintree. Mike was familiar with our music because he had already listened to the demo for a few months courtesy of Brian May. They got to hear us playing the songs live and discuss how we were going to re-record from 16 to 24 tracks. We got to meet under a controlled environment in Boston where we could become friends prior to going on to the great unknown of Los Angeles.

At the end of 1978 Infinity/MCA Records had a launching party at the Public Library in New York City. We pulled up and I counted at least another twenty limousines. It was like the Academy Awards. The guests of the evening were two bands, Orleans and New England. It was a marathon of introductions and shaking hands with the Infinity staff from all over North America. Just like my friends The Babys, we were there in brand suits from Barney's, watching presentation films of New England, and doing the business of getting our record promoted. We stayed at the Waldorf Astoria and in the morning everyone at the New York presentation flew on two leased airplanes to Los Angeles. There were two more days of the Infinity MCA records launch at Universal City and Century City.

Initially we stayed in Beverly Hills at L'Ermitage with our own suites. The coolest part was the phone in the bathroom– very rare in the 70s. We each made it a point to call everyone we knew from there. We then moved into the Oakwood Apartments on Woodman Avenue in Sherman Oaks. It was very near Laurel Canyon and a quick drive to the clubs on Sunset Boulevard in West Hollywood. We each got our own studio apartment and a few rental cars. In the pre cell phone days everyone got a new Los Angeles land line phone number and we felt very cool, each having a phone on both coasts.

After three days of parties and presentations in New York and Los Angeles, it was back to work as we began pre-production. Rehearsals were down the street in The Valley at a studio owned by Moose Orreckinto, a former KISS crew alumni. We got a lot of work done plotting how we were going to lay things down in the studio. Paul knew lots of musicians and every day someone like Carmine Apiece would pop by to say hi and cheer us on.

I went shopping one day on Rodeo Drive in Beverly Hills with Paul. We went into a men's store and he saw a really nice silk shirt that he wanted. He then decided to buy the shirt in 4 different colors. That wasn't impressive. What was very impressive was that he paid to have the shirts delivered to his hotel as he didn't want to carry bags around. It was good to be Paul.

We were now in the netherworld of fame that we dreamed of and worked so hard for.

The air got thinner and we entered an alternate reality where hat sizes enlarged and the career pitfalls increased. Hey man, love ya. My machine will call your machine. We'll do sushi. Ciao baby.

Finally, as autumn leaves became sleigh bells, we set up at Davlen Studios on Lankershim Boulevard in North Hollywood. Autumn leaves and sleigh bells in Los Angeles weren't quite the same for us coming from Boston but we gladly enjoyed the mild weather and Christmas decorations on palm trees.

Davlen was a very non-assuming one story building among many others. It didn't look like much from the outside, especially as we weren't far from MCA's high rise office headquarters of black glass called The Black Rock. I wasn't that familiar with Davlen when I entered the lobby. I found myself staring at over 30 gold and platinum albums that had been recorded there. Everyone from Fleetwood Mac to Toto to Barbara Streisand. The staff were used to high-profile clients and sensed something was happening with the presence of Paul Stanley and Mike Stone guiding an unknown band from out of town.

Hirsh and I began to cut the basic tracks of all the songs. I went directly into the board using my trusty 1965 Fender Jazz Bass. I had just received one of the last 1976 Bicentennial Thunderbird basses from the Gibson factory in Michigan, through Kenny Anderson's office in New York. I played the songs Last Show and Punk with it. John and Jimmy played scratch tracks as reference guides for us. Hirsh is a human metronome and rocked the tempos as we spun along with no problems. The songs began to build and take on life of their own. There were a few changes made. We had never recorded Shall I Run Away other than a home demo. The original arrangement was shortened by eliminating a long moody middle section featuring just John and Jimmy. I still miss it. You can compare the original to the new version on our Archives 5 CD box set on Cherry Red Records. The biggest change was on Don't Ever Wanna to Lose Ya. There was no guitar solo on the demo. Paul said, "It's a rock song. It's gotta have a blazing guitar solo." John was up for the occasion and cut a classic guitar solo. The great thing about John's solos is that he doesn't repeat them or just riff through the chord changes. Each solo is tailored to the song's melody. Also coming out of the solo Paul suggested a 'ba-bam' going into the final chorus. Once the basic tracks were finished, John and Jimmy could start laying on all their cool guitar and keyboard parts. With Mike's knowledge of the recording console and Paul's judgement on the perfect takes, it was all starting to sound really good. We had a steady stream of visitors from management and Infinity Records. Everyone was leaving with a smile on their face, telling us well done, keep going.

John is a great songwriter and I really enjoy the musical variety of New England songs. We can do the lighter songs like Conversation or the bombastic Seal It With A Kiss equally well. John produced a band years later who did an acoustic version of Don't Ever Wanna Lose Ya, and at one of our recent shows he asked what it was that I played on the choruses. I showed him the walking bass parts and also the last two bar licks at the end that were a homage to Chris Squire. It goes by very quickly and gets buried a bit by our big sound. I've never heard anyone play it correctly. He asked how I figured that out. I said, playing your songs is like the yellow pages, my fingers just do the walking." I`m very proud of my bass lines on songs like Hello Hello, Alone Tonight, and Shall I Run Away. I could play with power like my hero John Entwistle, or bouncy walking parts like Paul Mc Cartney. I played all of the New England albums with my fingers, and all of the Alcatrazz tracks with a pick for more grind and attack. I again encourage every beginning bass player to learn both styles.

We didn't work too late into the night, even though we had a 24 hour lockout. That left us time to relax in our apartments or go out and have decent meals. We spent many evenings at the Rainbow Bar and Grill, which actually had good food. Their steaks were good and the pizza was the best in the area back in the 70's. The clientele then was more music business and less tourist wasteland as it is today.

There was also time booked at Cherokee studios in Hollywood for extra dubs Journey was also in recording tracks and we met their singer Steve Perry, who was very affable and encouraging. We would open for Journey and ACDC the next summer, doing five shows together in Texas with them on our first North American tour. Across the street from Cherokee on Fairfax is the famous Oki Dog stand turning out tortillas with two large hot dogs, chili, a slice of cheese and pastrami wrapped in a burrito style. A massive gastronomic endeavor for those with a steely constitution.

By the end of December 1978 our work was done. We had recorded the basic tracks for our 10 songs. We had enough material to do a double album, but the consensus was to hold back on the extra songs. We released the Earmark Demos years later as a CD called

New England 1978. It's interesting to compare the demo to the album as they are pretty much the same except for a few tempos. I always chuckle when someone sees Paul's name on the album and they say that they can hear the "KISS influence." Really? Any similarity would be in our combined musical influences as we are all the same age. I loved it when Paul decided he had to sing background vocals on Don't Ever Wanna Lose Ya. You can hear his voice on the end of every verse .

We broke for the holidays and sent our gear back east with Hawkeye, our new road manager and ex KISS crew member. John stayed in Boston, I went to Connecticut, Hirsh went to Toronto, and Jimmy spent time in Wilmington, North Carolina. In mid-January of the new year we went to Electric Lady Studios in New York City, the home base of Jimi Hendrix and the studio built by Eddie Kramer. I stood across the street from the studio years before in Greenwich Village in awe, and now we were going to play music in this iconic musical fortress. Seven years later, Jimmy Waldo and I would work with Eddie again in Alcatrazz, with Steve Vai on guitar. The vocals were cut over the next two weeks and everything moved to Trident Studios in London to be mixed.

Chapter 13

The ensuing years were dream-like. We were so very fortunate to not only have a record with a major label, but also to be hailed by the major music business as being the next big thing. We made it into Billboard Magazine`s Top 40 charts. In a few months our record would be applauded as one of the Top Four Best Bands of 1979 by Circus Magazine. They listed The Knack, The Cars, New England, and Molly Hatchet, in that order. We ran the gauntlet through a career crushing system that has no sympathies. The only thing that soothed it was talent, grit, and money.

I'm sitting here writing this forty plus years later thinking wow, my friends and I went along the yellow brick road and were able to come back not so much with pockets full of gold, but a large amount of pride and a sense of achievement. The first New England album unlocked a series of major accomplishments that were heard around the world, setting up many opportunities for the four of us in the years to come.

Did you ever go to the circus and see the human cannonball get shot out of the huge gun? When you see a fighter jet get launched from an aircraft carrier catapult, what do you think is going through the pilot's mind? 1979 was the year we were tutored and coached by Rick Aliberte and Gail Rogers in all things promotion at Aucoin Management / Rock Steady Productions in New York City. Bill Aucoin and Sean Delaney showed us the ways to move on an arena stage. We were taught how to give interviews, how to give live on the air short answers, how to do station IDs, as well as how to do an autograph signing at a record store. We were launched into the annals of rock and roll history.

It was a very busy year, starting with our new album release, a sixty-five city North American tour, and the recording of our second album at the end of the year. On January 11th, we were flown down to New York City by Peter Corriston, art director for Infinity Records. He had hired photographer Andre Holusca, who wanted us to take photos for the album cover in the bathroom of the St. Regis Hotel. He liked the tile color. I had mentioned to Rick Aliberte and Bill Aucoin about the forces of the weather in New England being a good concept for the album cover art. Both being from Massachusetts they got it. Andre's idea was to have a blurry picture of us since we are so mysterious. When we saw the blurred photo, we immediately vetoed it. We had a decent looking band and this was just stupid. If you look at the album cover, there is a photo behind the main photo. I am the face on the left and Jimmy is in the upper right hand corner of the blurry photo. Because of our protest, Infinity Records sent a well-known fashion photographer, Alec Mac Weeny, to shoot a good photo of us in Boston two weeks later. We used both photos overlapping each other, hence the weird photo art. The name in the four corners is supposed to represent North, East, South and West. The name couldn't be any smaller. Needless to say, we thought it was very underwhelming in the world of great album cover art.

John and Jimmy had returned from London with the Trident Studios mixes and they sounded great. A listening party for the media was arranged and held at the Hit Factory Recording studio in Manhattan. Lew Wasserman, President for the MCA group in L.A., sent Ron Alexenburg a letter giving us the highest praise for our new album. In April Infinity wanted to do a launch party in Boston at Quincy market. All good until we heard

Ron wanted us to play live. We hadn't played live in two years and our gear, augmented with our new gear, was not ready to be moved. We are probably the first and last band to play Quincy Market. It's an old colonial granite warehouse with horrible acoustics. We played, it was loud and brash to our ears, but everyone was happy. WCOZ FM DJ Bob Slaven was the first to play our record on the radio that night and it sounded great.

    Next up was a promo trip to Toronto, Canada with radio personalities and program directors CHOM FM and Montreal's, CHUM FM. Infinity Canada's record promotion team and Ric led the charge. We rented an exotic car dealership at Greene Motors in Toronto and had our albums coming out of the trunks of Ferraris and Lamborghinis in the showroom. Convention models walked around serving hors d`oeuvres. Our only mission was to party hard with Canada's foremost disc jockeys and did we ever. The champagne was flowing and there was a second party going on in the manager's office where everyone was sniffling with allergy-like symptoms. We raised hell into the wee hours, keeping the Yorkville neighbors awake with our celebration and new friends. May 7th we began rehearsing at Britt Row Rehearsal Studios in Long Island City. It was Pink Floyd's North American headquarters. KISS was there rehearsing for the Dynasty Tour and we were on another stage. Bill Aucoin's partner, Sean Delaney, worked with us as a true stage drill sergeant. We had state-of-the-art video cameras to work with. We would watch them back and work on bad stage moves. "Look how dumb you look, look, you did it again." Sean emphatically emphasized that John and I, being out in front of the band, needed to exaggerate even more when we made any gestures so it could be seen from the fortieth row of an arena. This was in preparation for our upcoming gigs at The Pontiac Silver Dome in Detroit and the Omni in Atlanta.

In mid-May, we were at Unitel Film Studios in New York City to shoot two videos. The studio shot hundreds of television commercials. We did a video for "Lose Ya" and one for the song ""It was an early time in music video history. Most bands didn't have one. Usually if someone had a video they were famous like Queen or Elton John. For us to have one so early in our career was a big deal.

At the end of May, we left our second home at the infamous Gorham Hotel in midtown Manhattan and headed to Albany on our first tour bus. We did eight concerts with The Outlaws in the Northeast, ending with a show at The Cape Cod Coliseum. They were very good to us and we became fast friends with their lead guitarist, Freddie Salem. We went back to Boston and played a home game, headlining at the Paradise Theater. The after show party at my apartment, a mile away, was an award winner.

The next week we flew to Denver and sold out The Rainbow Theater, getting three encores as we taped a live show for Denver's KAZY F M. Another flight to Seattle brought us to a sold-out show at the Paramount Theater. Two shows were broadcast in San Francisco on KSANFM, and we did a sold-out show at the Santa Monica Civic Center with KLOS FM. We then found ourselves in Phoenix Arizona at Dully's, where my friend Bill Buckland got to see the revamped Fatback that he had seen years before.

Chapter 14

All of our hard work was going to pay off, as now we hooked-up with Journey and ACDC for five shows in Texas. We played the Sam Houston Coliseum, Austin, San Antonio, Corpus Christi, and Dallas. Steve Perry said they had our record on their bus and loved it. He said it took Journey a half hour into their set to get the crowd into a second wind after both our bands had gone before them. Journey hired Mike Stone after this to produce their next record. Our tour took us to Kansas City and St. Louis. We played The Park West in Chicago and broadcast live to 13 states.

Three days later, at the beginning of July, we went to Hampton Coliseum, in Hampton, Virginia to start a tour of over twenty concerts on the KISS Dynasty Tour. We played together until the end of August. The biggest moment of the tour was two nights at Madison Square Garden. Playing in front of KISS in New York City is a challenge for any band. We got an encore at both shows. My friend Jerry Talbot was there with me as our guitar tech. I was glowing all over thinking about my high school principal Lawrence D`Angelo giving me a hard time in high school, as I leaned against my wall of bass amplifiers. We played the Montreal Forum and another great moment arose. Canada has a Canadian Content Law for radio and since Hirsh was Canadian, we received lots of airplay. Our promo weekend in Toronto had paid off: We got a standing ovation before we played the first song. The crowd roared like Montreal had just scored a goal in game seven of the Stanley Cup Finals. John and I were dumbfounded, so was Gene Simmons.

At the end of our time on the Dynasty Tour we headed to Minneapolis for half a dozen shows with Styx. We did the Milwaukee Summerfest, Minnesota State Fair, and two nights at the Michigan State Fair in Detroit. We did a one-off show with Rush in Lansing. Our crew had built a stand that could hold an Ovation acoustic guitar for John out of a Hirsh's pile of broken drum hardware that laid in the corner of the studio. There was nothing like it on the market in those days. Geddy Lee and Alex Liefson marveled at it during our soundcheck. They wanted one and were impressed that we had made it ourselves. That night they headlined, but we got the loudest crowd response when we played Lose Ya.

For the next album, Explorer Suite, we made some major changes. We wanted to record in Boston with John co-producing with Mike Stone. Michael agreed as long as he could ship extra gear from London to Intermediate Studios on Newbury street. He would also bring his assistant, John Brand. We played some new material in Braintree for Infinity and started recording from mid-October to late December. Another big change was that from now on, all of our crew were going to be residents of Boston. No more crew personnel from out of state spending money on hotels and rental cars. We sat around the studio TV one night and watched our video of Lose Ya play on Don Kirshner's Rock Concert show. We were beside ourselves screaming and cheering.

The best made plans of mice and men would become an apt refrain again. The phone rang a few days later, and we learned that Infinity does not mean forever. They had spent a fortune signing the Pope to a record deal, and its parent company, MCA, had pulled the plug. The good news was that there were forty-four bands on the Infinity roster and MCA decided to keep four. We were one of those four. So much for Ron Alexenburg's big sell to us about only taking on a few bands and working closely with them.

It was a great Christmas in 1979. December 27th was my 29th birthday. It had been quite a year of activity heading into the 80's. The new decade brought us some major changes. New England had a new album and a new label. We spun the roulette wheel, hoping one more time to beat the house. We released Explorer Suite, a story of a young boy awaiting his astronaut father's return. It was a new spin on the centuries-old story of those that hoped their loved ones would return from a life at sea, whether a ship's captain, or a cabin boy.

The first week of January we all flew to Los Angeles to meet MCA Records President Bob Siner. We talked about label support, artwork, and enthusiasm. Bob said he was prepared to do his best for us. MCA stands for The Music Corporation of The World. No fresh upstart there. That evening we were wined and dined by Kenny Batista of Elektra Records. He told us they were still very interested in us and again called us the American Queen that they were looking for. We returned to the East Coast and a few days later the consensus was unanimous for signing with Electra.

The next hurdle was an overwhelming opinion that the new mixes could sound better. The band was booked January 15th through 30th into the Gorham Hotel and Media Studios in Manhattan for a remix. We had one of the three studios blocked out. The other two clients were the Ian Hunter Band and James Brown. Michael had his playback system for maximum effect. It was convenient for everyone concerned that the whole team was in New York, and communication was instantaneous. We were just a few blocks from the Aucoin office. I enjoyed talking to Ian Hunter about our mutual friend Luther Grosvenor a.k.a. Ariel Bender. One day I stepped out of the hallway to clear my ears and there was James Brown, standing there doing the same thing. He was also mixing an album. I`ve never been one to ask a celebrity for a photo with anyone. I asked Mr. Brown if he would mind if I had my picture taken with him, he replied, "Sure son." I couldn't believe it, as I put on a huge grin.

The mixes were reworked and everything moved along. On March 7th, MCA released us from our contract and we were free to go with Electra. Oh Elektra, let the storm clouds begin. We retained music lawyer Brian Rohan in San Francisco to negotiate with Elektra. Once again there was more talking about the Red Sox than moving quickly with business and less expensively. There was a song called Conversation that we all agreed should be the single. It was an acoustic "Cruel To Be Kind" type of song in the midst of New Wave artists like The Clash, Pretenders, and Elvis Costello. Elektra, in their lack of wisdom, chose our big production track Explore Suite, saying it showcased the band's musicality. They tried to unsuccessfully edit it down for time with outside engineers. When it came out, the radio stations around the country said we were dinosaurs and would not add it to their playlists. Thank you, Elektra.

The album was released on October 17th. We had lost valuable time being off the road. We had played a dozen local gigs and rehearsed on our full schedule, and we were ready to go on our next North American tour. In late November, we left Boston for Mobile Alabama during Thanksgiving and hooked up with Kansas for a half dozen shows. We had an underwhelming Thanksgiving dinner together in a roadside truck stop halfway there. In the coming month we would play shows with Cheap Trick, Humble Pie, Thin Lizzy, John Cougar Mellencamp, Ronnie Montrose, and Blue Oyster Cult.

We had two shows booked at The Warehouse in New Orleans and Dallas with Thin Lizzy. The Warehouse was a famous venue but was due to stop hosting concerts. The bill was Thin Lizzy, Special Guest, New England, and the opening act was a new wave band from L.A. called Code Blue. When we arrived for a sound check we were told by Thin

Lizzie's tour manager that they wanted us to go on first. We asked why? They said the set change would be faster, as one of their guitarists had his leg in a cast. Our reply was that we were the special guest and that it was an insult to our crew who could strike our gear in 10 minutes. The guys in Code Blue pleaded to go on first, as they, being a new wave band, were not going over very well with Thin Lizzy fans. The argument went back-and-forth. We agreed to the demand since we had two shows together. They opened the doors in the middle of our sound check. We went out and did our set and with eight minutes to go. Suddenly they turned the house lights on saying 'that was it' before we could play Lose Ya. We went back on stage and John asked the crowd with the lights up, do you want to hear more? The crowd cheered. The lights dimmed eventually. We finished our song and left the building. The two bands passed each other later that night in the tight quarters of The Crow's Nest, in the French Quarter. No one spoke and there was no confrontation.

The next day in Dallas, we were doing a band interview in my hotel room with the Dallas Times. I called the gig to see what time the band should leave for a sound check. Our crew informed us we weren't playing and there were signs saying one of us was sick. I asked the band if anyone was sick and of course the answer was no. Without any communication, Thin Lizzy was again being hard to deal with. There was an anniversary party that night for a rock magazine called Buddy Magazine. All three bands were invited. We got there first. Code Blue came in and said a beer bottle was thrown at them, smashing on the guitarist's Stratocaster. They were very upset. In came Thin Lizzie. Our friend from the Dallas Times went up to Thin Lizzy's leader, Phil Lynott, with his tape recorder on and asked why New England was bumped off the bill. He said he had two reasons. I jumped up and said, "Let's hear it, A and B." He proceeded to say that his band was breaking up, unknown to the public. He told us they had not heard of us, but when they saw our truck open with gear like Pink Floyd, they freaked out. He admitted they had wronged us, saying with a smile, 'you guys are a great band, take it as a left hand compliment, we screwed you around.' We shook hands. Both bands went to the bar together for drinks as road touring friends.

Situations like this rarely arose for us, and we treated all bands opening for us graciously. I will say that there were three other bands guilty of stage sabotage. They would be Blue Oyster Cult, April Wine, and the lovely Johnny Cougar Mellencamp. It's interesting how all four of these incidents happened on our second tour. These artists had problems with KISS and took it out on us by association. This was our FOAD Tour. F*** Off And Die. We weren't taking flak from anyone, and flung it right back at them.

Chapter 15

We played in St. Paul, Minnesota, in a brand new civic center with Cheap Trick. There was a snowstorm going on and we had more people at the sound check than there were at the evening's concert. The facility was great, the staff were super, and we'd played one of our tightest sets yet. We got off the stage feeling victorious. Our sound man, Paul Correlli, showed us a very negative review in the local paper. The writer said yet another band that will need a dozen tape recorders to play live. We asked who this guy was. We were told by local staff at the radio station he was sitting out in the hallway on a road case. His name was John Bream, and he was a big Bob Dylan fan. John and Jimmy went out, introduced themselves and asked if he had seen the show. He said no. They asked if he had listened to the advance album that Elektra Records had sent him. He said no. John poured a full beer over his head asking then why did you write this then? Jimmy took the pencils out of his pocket, breaking them saying here's what we think of your "journalism". Rick Nielsen and Robin Zander were nearby and couldn't contain their laughter.

The next day at breakfast we read his new article, saying that he had never been assaulted by a rock band before. He claimed he had confused us with the band Nantucket from North Carolina and had newfound respect for us, standing up for ourselves. We left town being added to the regular rotation on the local F.M. station, which wasn't the case before we played there.

New England came back for the missed show in Dallas a month later and set a house attendance record at The Dallas Agora, besting a previous record set by Cheap Trick. My great friend Charlie Early and I used to drive around Litchfield County Connecticut in his Austin Healey 3000 in the late 60s. He had an 8-track tape player in the car and two sets of headphones. We would drive for miles on end through the beautiful countryside just enjoying listening to music. One of our favorite tapes was The Nazz, Todd Rundgren's band from Philadelphia. I thought how lucky I would be if I could join a band like that someday. When my friend Bill Buckland told me of the band Fatback he had seen, he said they did a long version of the Nazz song Under The Ice. The members of New England all had that Nazz common thread. The great thing is that we all enjoy the same style of music.

The beginning of 1981 found us resuming our North American Tour. We played headline dates around the Midwest in Detroit and Chicago. In mid-January we drove to Dayton, Ohio to begin a ten city tour of Canada and the Great Plains with Molly Hatchet. The snow was deep and the temperatures were freezing. From Dayton we played through Green Bay, Fargo, Bismarck, Winnipeg, Calgary, Edmonton, Denver, Grand River Junction, and Salt Lake City. The guys in Molly Hatchet were terrific, and took me repelling from the main beam of the arenas with them. The game was to go upside down and stop as your ponytail touched the floor. At our last show together, they dropped hundreds of ping pong balls from the ceiling on us. Balls everywhere. I got to go up on their stage during their final song dressed as a Viking on a fake horse manned by John Fannon and Toby Fleming on our last night in Salt Lake City. That really surprised them and they loved it. We also gave them an engraved hatchet from us that we had custom made at the previous show in Denver.

From Salt Lake City we did shows in Illinois, Michigan, and Ohio. At the end of the tour, we played with April Wine in Kansas City, and as special guests with Loverboy as the opening act. April Wine pulled the 'Times Up' trick on us, cutting our set short on time left. A few years later, Jimmy and I would play in Puerto Rico with Loverboy again as Alcatrazz.

We were ready to begin recording our third album called Walking Wild. It was our second record for Elektra, and we were very wary as to what damage they could do to us this time. We didn't need to wait too long to find out. The band decided we wanted a producer/musician who could do it all and maybe come up with something very special. We wanted someone who knew how to play music as well as do magic with the recording console. Our choice was Todd Rundgren. The four of us were serious Nazz fans. Todd had done great work on his own solo records, his band Utopia, Grand Funk Railroad, The Tubes, and Meatloaf. He was available and offered for us to come to his home studio near Woodstock, New York. We were excited that he said yes. What was interesting was that all of our new material was incomplete, and some would be brand new.

We left for Todd's on March 6th and planned on meeting him and his engineer, Chris, the next day. We drove a rental car up a leafy two track road in the woods called Mink Hollow. Suddenly a black Jeep came barreling down the hill towards us. It was Todd and Chris. We all got out in the woods and shook hands. Todd's studio was in an A frame building on his property, near his main house. The instruments were spread around the floor of the studio, and the recording console was up in a glassed-off loft, complete with a four poster bed. We couldn't go up to the main house because his wife just had a baby. The studio was very comfortable and surrounded by woods, very much like our own place in Braintree.

The day after our initial meeting, we drove to Utopia's warehouse in nearby Poughkeepsie, New York. It was near the Hudson River and housed all of Utopia's gear and props from previous tours. Some of it was familiar, as I had seen the original six piece Utopia play at The Cape Cod Coliseum. Since most of our material was rough and unfinished, we set up a schedule. We'd work on the tracks and Todd would come in and out checking our progress and offering suggestions. It was a whole different way of working on the new songs. Todd was the deciding fifth voice and we listened and learned his style of making music. We all thought the track Walking Wild could be a hit dance song.

One week later we moved into Todd's studio and began cutting basic tracks. I had brought a few bases along and asked which one he wanted me to play. He asked which one was my favorite, and I showed him my 1965 Fender jazz bass. He said plug it in. Mike Stone had urged me to buy a new Music Man bass on the last album. I used it but didn't like it and sold it immediately after the Explorer Suite basic tracks were finished. We were about to play hardball in the studio and complete final tracks and final mixes within the next two weeks. No challenge there. Todd was easy to work with and had a great sense of humor.

John had another song about space and was hung up on the lyrics. Todd took a notepad and sat on the studio stairs. In less than 20 minutes he wrote the lyrics to L5. It's about coordinates in space that Timothy Leary and Buckminster Fuller thought would be a good place for a space station. The song Don't Ever Let Me Go was recorded to be a follow-up to Don't Ever Wanna Lose Ya. It had lots of singing, and the icing on the cake was that Todd played a harmony guitar part with John on the solo. We were geeked about the lead guitarist from Nazz playing on our record. We worked quickly on the music.

When the harmony singing came, Todd got very serious with great vocal ideas. Everyone sang great.

Another song with no lyrics was tentatively titled Stay With Me Tonight. Todd said Rod Stewart already did that, and he thought for a minute and said how about something like be my dirty dream tonight? Then he said, laughing, we can call it DDT. We all thought that was a great idea to liven things up and have some fun. A mix was sent to the office of Elektra in Los Angeles. The response was that the staff were dancing on their desks and that it was definitely a hit song. The band was super tight. We finished up right on schedule in three weeks and we all drank champagne together. Todd's parting words were, No matter what you do, don't let Elektra f*** this up.

Good old Goddess Elektra, bring the storm clouds on. They released DDT over our better judgment as our first single. Every female music director and program director in America said we were male chauvinist pigs, refusing to play the record. We got no airplay.

A few months after the album was released, Elektra Records dropped us.

On Todd's current tour he plays a video montage of the groups he's worked with behind him. Great to see New England up there. Once again, Elektra Records let us down. They had personnel changes, an explosion of new wave bands, and no one was going to bat for us as promised. Bill and Ric did all they could to light fires under people in Los Angeles, but to no avail. Ric had even been an Elektra Asylum Records promotion man. Unfortunately for us, we caught them at a bad time. Another setback was our booking agency in New York City, American Talent International, telling us that they didn't book colleges, only major tours. There are over 250 colleges in New England and we decided to seek booking elsewhere.

We approached an old ally, Howie Cusack, at Pretty Polly Productions in Boston to help us secure bookings in the college market. Not only did they take care of us, but the bookings did well for us. From the release of Explorer Suite in May 1981, we worked constantly on the college circuit. We played the University of Maine in Augusta, with The Ramones, and shows at The Orpheum Theater in Boston with Nazareth, and other shows with The Joe Perry project. We also did a 15 city East Coast tour with Foghat between Boston and Virginia Beach. My mom got to see us at the New Haven Coliseum. It was a long way back to the days when we were rehearsing in our attic as The Insane.

Another cool thing about The New Haven Coliseum show was that all three bass players were from Connecticut that night. Foghat was an English band but their new bassist was Craig McGregor from the New Haven area. The Joe Perry project was added to that show. David Hull, their bass player who had been a member of the Buddy Miles Express and has been a touring member of Aerosmith, was from Stratford, Connecticut.

We had called Todd after we left Elektra and he said he would do another album with us. The band was working on a dozen new songs at the Braintree studio, and we would play one or two colleges on the weekends. We had fine-tuned our road trips, so nothing was more than two hours by car. For the first time we were moving out of debt and operating in the black. We had no worries about getting another label. The unreleased tracks can be found on our 5 cd box set on Cherry Red Records.

One day of the clear blue, John walked into rehearsal and said he was leaving the band for personal reasons after our current bookings were done. To say we went into shock is an understatement. The best made plans of mice and men. The three of us were road dogs and liked to play live and travel. John expressed that he wanted to move to Beverly Hills to write music for movies and be a producer. He told me I was immature for wanting to play heavy rock in arenas. I bit my lip pretending I hadn't heard that. He said he wanted to start a family and didn't like touring. I understood that, but we were in our early thirties. To say we were beyond angry and let down is also an understatement.

The friction would last the next twenty years. Fortunately for us, our friendship bound us together again with new music in a new century and live shows on both the East and West coasts and a show in Japan. Big thanks to the New England Nation. The last remaining shows we had booked in 1983 were over and all went amicably, like nothing had changed. John took his gear and we said to ourselves how hard it would be to replace him, as a guitarist, singer, and songwriter. That's hard to find among any musician. We immediately put out the word to all our friends at guitar companies and music stores seeking a new guitarist.

Chapter 16

An interesting list of guitarists called and said they were definitely intrigued. This is a partial list: Charlie Huhn of Ted Nugent, Cary Sharaf of Billy Squire, Mike Slammer from the band City Boy, and Neil Geraldo from Rick Derringer. Gene Simmons told us of a guitarist who filled all our requirements. He told us there was a great guitarist/writer that they were working with in the studio in Los Angeles. Unfortunately, Gene said, the guy was too short to replace Ace Frehley and gave us his phone number.

We received a demo tape from Vinnie Cusano, originally from Bridgeport Connecticut. He had an impressive resume and had played for Laura Nyro, Dan Hartman, Felix Cavaliere from The Rascals, and was a staff writer for the TV show Happy Days. The music on the tape was different from New England but we all agreed it really rocked and was definitely radio friendly.

Vinnie flew to Boston. We picked him up at the airport and drove straight to our studio in Braintree. We told him what we were looking for but didn't tell him we had learned his demo songs. He plugged in and it was interesting hearing a new twist on our music. When we were done, we congratulated him on a job well done. We then proceeded to play songs of his and he blew his mind. He said how amazing it sounded and how he couldn't find guys like us in Los Angeles. Where had we heard that before? The four of us sat around knowing we had something cool going on and decided to sleep on it. The next day we played together again and started to figure out a game plan.

Vinnie was co-writing with KISS. If he got his songs on their album, it would be tremendous as his wife had just given birth to twin girls. It would be hard to travel back and forth between Los Angeles and Boston for all of us, but a solution was devised. What if we abandoned the New England legacy all together to see if we could start a whole new band in Los Angeles? Vinnie had a lawyer friend who would fund some rehearsal time and Jimmy had an aunt in Covina with a big house where we could stay for free, complete with a car.

So began the beginning of a new band tentatively named Warrior. It rose out of the ashes of New England, which would become dormant for the next 20 years. Once more I decided to keep my apartment in Brookline until the smoke cleared and everything was running smoothly. We began rehearsing at SIR studios on Sunset Blvd and going through Vinnie's songs. He didn't feel like singing and playing lead guitar at the same time so we were looking for a singer also. We worked in the daytime, and Vinnie worked with KISS at the Record Plant at night.

Fergie Frederickson, who had success with Le Roux, came in to sing. He would later join Toto. Fergie fit right in, but he also wanted to audition for Angel. I had rented an Acoustic 360 bass amp that was beat-up and sounded outstanding. It sounded like a freight train. I taped the rehearsals daily with my Sony Walkman Pro to listen to my playing. It was turned directly toward my amp, so the mix is very uneven. Not much guitar. These tapes would eventually end up on a Warrior CD containing recording demos and live rehearsals.

It wasn't long before KISS changed their minds and made Vinnie an offer he couldn't refuse. They knew his talent and they wanted his songs. Would you like to make a few thousand dollars a week with KISS, or hope that this new band would eventually take off? Obviously, Vinnie took the deal and became Vinnie Vincent.

I will say that Vinnie was a great guitarist at this time. Very cool. He sang like Lou Graham and his guitar playing was very funky and melodic– much like Jeff Beck. It's sad that he tried to become a shredder and go way overboard, eventually getting let go from KISS. At one point he had the world in his hands, but he let his insecurities get the better of him and he flamed out.

Once again it was back to the drawing board. I was in my early 30's and thought maybe we had been lucky with New England and that was it. This was a moment of sink or swim, where many people give up their dreams for another career– possibly easier or up to others' expectations. Some would say, "Oh I couldn't make any money at it." Newsflash: You play guitar to make music, and I believe that if you love it enough, it will carry you through the rough spots. My apartment was still there in Boston but there was nothing there to offer me musically. I knew if I was to continue in music it would have to be in Los Angeles where there were more opportunities. Hirsh opted to stay close to home in Boston while Jimmy and I definitively decided to move to Los Angeles. We didn't know that a whole new music scene in L.A. was about to explode there. I finally left my cozy Victorian aerie in Boston after 10 years. There were many great times and memories there. I was nostalgic in one way, but optimistic for new adventures. Little did I know that I would be a founding member of another iconic band, and a father of three great kids.

In Los Angeles I spent time with my good friend, Jon Hyde, the drummer of Detective. I went around to a rehearsal space he had and jammed with him and various guitarists. One of them was Jamie Herndon, who played guitar on Nick Gilder's Hot Child In The City. He was experimenting with guitar synthesizers and we made some interesting pieces of music. I told Michael Monarch that I had placed an ad in the paper looking for a gig and he said all I would get would be calls from crazies. I said well, I'm placing an ad in the paper and covering all bases. I also reminded him that an ad in a newspaper had brought us together in London a few years before. My ad read, ex name bass player seeks rock group or recording project. I got about 75 calls of mostly amateur musicians just starting out.

I was getting ready to go out on a Friday night when the phone rang and a loud booming voice with a Midlands English accent asked, "Are you a bass player? Well, who are you?" I explained that he may never have heard of New England. He said you were backstage at an Electric Light Orchestra show eating all the shrimp in Providence, Rhode Island last year. I said yes, but not so much for the shrimp part. He explained he was Andy Truman and that he had worked with ELO, Jethro Tull, The Bay City Rollers, and Robert Palmer. This call got my attention. The voice said he was looking to put a band together for his neighbor Graham Bonnet of Rainbow, with Barrymore Barlow from Jethro Tull, and Zal Clemson from Nazareth. He asked me, "Are you the bass player?" I confidently said yes. He said it would be a true band rather than a backup band as Graham didn't want all of the work and responsibility of that. Also, he asked if I knew a keyboard player. I said I'd let him know.

I called Jimmy who lived less than a mile from me in West Hollywood and told him of my conversation with Andy. I talked again to Andy and told him about Jimmy. He thought it was a good feature that the two of us had already played together. Andy mentioned that Graham was very hard to work with, but he was prepared to see this group through regardless. It was one of Andy's more truthful comments and a harbinger of things to come.

On Sunday March 13th, 1983, the four of us agreed to meet at the Hyatt House on Sunset Boulevard. The famous 'Riot House' of Led Zeppelin legend. Jimmy and I had liked what Graham had sung in Rainbow and Michael Schenker. We had not yet heard all of the horror stories of why he was not in either band any longer. Although Graham had no idea who we were, we talked about starting a band in a similar vein of music. We felt we had a good combination of people and we could make a fresh start of things. Andy had said that Barry Barlow and guitarist Zal Clemson were part of this new band and would join us soon in Los Angeles.

Bob Sifkin was a good friend of mine and Jimmy's through the band New England. He was director of Artists and Repertoire for MCA Records. He was also a neighbor of Andy's. Bob told us of a new label called Rocshire Records that he thought we should look into. They were new and well-funded and had recently reached a distribution deal with MCA. Andy was a master salesman and could sell ice cubes to the polar bears. He took meetings with Rocshire's President, Rocky Davis. Andy convinced him that he should not pass up signing this new super band.

Rocshire was down in Orange County, an hour south of Los Angeles in a commercial park. There was an office complex, a 24 track studio, and a state of the art rehearsal studio, all in separate buildings. Andy sensed big investors and talked Rocky into signing us just on our previous track records. Rocky agreed. Again, to set a major Internet Fallacy straight, we recorded no demos for the first Alcatrazz album. Any instrumental recordings of the first album were done at rehearsal after the album was recorded.

Chapter 17

In April, myself, Graham, and Jimmy began rehearsing in Graham's garage in Calabasas, a true garage band. We had to wait until then, as Graham's wife Jo had just given birth to twins. We rehearsed some of Graham's ideas, like General Hospital and a song Jimmy had written for New England called Take Another Ride. Graham said he liked the Motown feel of it, and it became the song Island In The Sun. Barrymore called Andy saying he had a chance to play on Robert Plant's new solo album and he would be staying in England. Zal was on tour with Elke Brooks and there was no communication. We had to find two new band members immediately.

On May 21st, we set up at Diamond Sound in Chatsworth and auditioned Laurence Jubar from Paul McCartney's band, and drummer Robert Williams from Captain Beefheart's band. Needless to say, Laurence was an outstanding guitarist, but not right for us. We used the Russ Ballard song SOS that Graham had recorded on a solo album for the auditions. The same was true for Robert, who was a great drummer with many solo albums to his credit, but not the drummer we were looking for. Andy started raving how he could sell Rainbow, Wings, and New England. We all said no way, wrong guy. He asked around a record store the next day as to who was a hot guitar player. The reply was Yngwie Malmsteen, a young Swedish guitarist who had recently come to town. Yngwie came in and was totally devoted to the guitar style of Richie Blackmore and Uli Roth. Robert was a nice guy and had stayed the extra night on drums to help us out. All of a sudden, we sounded like the band we had imagined.

On May 26th, we moved into the Rocshire Records rehearsal facility to audition drummers. We played with Aynsley Dunbar from Journey, Bill Lordan from Robin Trower, Jon Hyde from Detective, Ed Cassidy from Spirit, and Clyde Burr from Iron Maiden over the course of three weeks. Another Internet Fallacy is that Clive Burr joined the band. I was there. He only auditioned for us for one day and we all decided to pass on him. We chose Jan Uvena from Alice Cooper's band the following week. We now had the correct lineup and proceeded to make a memorable album called "No Parole".

The subject of what to name ourselves came down to the wire. Yngwie wanted to call the band Excalibur and go the Dungeons & Dragons route. We listened, but that was not what we had in mind. I was saying one day that New England got stuck in the middle section of record stores between New Riders Of The Purple Sage and Olivia Newton John, where no one ever looked. I suggested that it would be cool to have a one-word name starting with the letter A, something like ABBA or ACDC, then the word Alcatraz just popped out of my mouth. Everyone agreed that it was cool. Andy said I was brilliant, and we immediately started saying slogans like No Parole, Disturbing The Peace, Parole Denied, etc. I not only helped start a great band, I named it as well.

In July we went to Alcatraz Island in San Francisco Bay for promo photography. We decided to add the extra Z to the name like jazz or nazz, to set us apart from the State of California. The extra Z also looks cooler. We got to see parts of the prison the tourists don't get to see. On our return we signed the Rocshire Records deal. We had been thinking about producers and a few names came up. We thought about Andy Johns. We knew he could record the big sound we were producing live at the time. His resume was outstanding, but he had some personal issues going on and we shied away. Looking back, we should have taken the risk. Dennis MacKay was chosen as he had worked with Jeff Beck and Al Dimeloa. Yngwie was a huge Al Dimeola fan at the time but would never admit it.

We began recording on July 14, 1983. We immediately ran into a problem. Dennis wanted to use the new electronic Syndrums. Most of the drum basic tracks had been recorded like this, but Jan and the band protested. Their sound was really popular on MTV at the time with the new synthesizer bands. The Syndrums didn't sound right, plus it was like drumming on a tabletop. All the songs were recut with Jan's acoustic drums. The recording went along smoothly into early September, as the band was well-rehearsed.

A friend of Vinnie Vincent once mentioned to me that Clint Eastwood had built a set for the Escape from Alcatraz movie and that it was still in operation in Culver City. We went to GMT Studios in Culver City and struck gold. The film studio was in full professional operation doing numerous police television shows and movies. It had a perfect replica of Alcatraz cell block C. In mid-October we teamed up with video director Michael Miner who had just helped write the hit movie Robocop. We were able to shoot Island In The Sun and Hiroshima Mon Amour in two days. We saved major money not having to fly everything and everyone to San Francisco. Once again, Andy said I was a genius. Jimmy, Andy, myself, and our road manager, Jake Duncan, began planning out our touring budgets and objectives. Unlike successful singers like Ronnie Dio or David Coverdale, Graham took no interest in production meetings or any type of budget strategy, preferring to just sing his parts and go home. This would never change.

S.I.R. rehearsals began in Hollywood in early November for some up-and-coming warm-up gigs. There was a very important show at the Country Club in Reseda booked, which would be recorded live and broadcast by the RKO Radio Network. Graham was very nervous about playing live again. Just as we were about to do our debut, Graham came down with Bell's Palsy and lost control of the muscles in his face. He couldn't sing. It was decided that acupuncture would help and I was elected to drive him around to all his therapy appointments. We postponed our gigs and waited. Within a month the condition improved and his muscle control returned. We played the Country Club on December 8th live over the RKO Radio Network, hosted by Jim Ladd. The show was a resounding success. It was recorded and was made into a live promo LP.

We left two weeks later for seven midwestern shows with Eddie Money and Saga as special guests. On New Year's Eve, we played in Cleveland at the Ridgefield Coliseum, a venue that Jimmy and I had played previously with New England. The arena was filling up with people ready to party and ring in the New Year. With two songs left to go, Graham, who had been drinking, came up to me saying he couldn't hear himself and ran off the stage, disappearing into the dark. Eddie Money's sound system was from one of the best sound companies in the world. It sounded great on stage. I went over to Yngwie and said solo time. None of us could believe what was happening. We played the last two songs instrumentally while the crowd scratched their heads, wondering what was going on. When we were done, we ran to our dressing room and Yngwie clocked Graham in the head with his fist. Jimmy was winding up for round two and Andy blocked his swing. There was much yelling and screaming. We got Graham back to his hotel room and put him to bed. The next day we found out Graham had two broken ribs from going right off the back of the stage and falling 15 feet, landing on road cases in the dark, rather than using the stairs. Happy New Year to us 1984.

On January 21st, 1984, we left for a headlining tour of Japan playing Tokyo, Osaka, and Nagoya. We were awarded a gold record for sales in Japan by our label Polydor. The fans were amazing and the shows were on fire. It was here that Yngwie started acting up after seeing signs that read 'Alcatrazz featuring Yngwie Malmsteen'. Andy was filling his head and ego with a lot of garbage, and he began running all over the stage, showing off. Graham was more than angry. We filmed a live concert, and Andy told the film crew to only concentrate on Graham and Yngwie. When Graham watched it, he threw the copy against the wall. We also recorded this as a live album which became Live Sentence. Yngwie was offered a four song EP by our label Polygram as being part of Alcatrazz. On the way home from Japan, we played a sold out show at The University of Hawaii. When we returned, Graham said he wanted Yngwie out of the band rather than him working harder within the band and taking control of the situation.

On February 2nd, the band went on a headlining tour of 19 shows in the Southwest, and a half dozen shows with Night Ranger in the West. Upon our return on March 30th, we started looking to replace Yngwie. Jimmy had talked to Rainbow keyboardist David Rosenthal, who had suggested Steve Vai from Frank Zappa's band. They had been friends since their days in music school in Boston. Yngwie was told he could stay home on May 5th, as nothing was happening. Meanwhile, we set up our entire backline at Studio A at Burbank Studios. We auditioned Steve and Chris Impellitteri, who was also a great guitarist and friend. Chris had the Blackmore/Roth style down cold, but Steve had a quirky originality about him that we liked. We asked Steve to join the band for our next record and he said yes.

We embarked on a fifty-one city tour on Ted Nugent's Penetrator Tour across America for most of the summer. Ted was very cordial to us and the shows all ran well. Midway through, Graham told us he was going home to Los Angeles after seeing a doctor at a hospital in Memphis. He said they diagnosed him with Multiple Sclerosis. We asked the Doctor if drinking two six packs of beer, a bottle of Robitusson, a bottle of aspirin, a bottle of throat spray, and smoking every day would have the same symptoms. He said yes. Graham finished the tour and never got MS.

Chapter 18

Internet fallacy: Graham purposefully stepped on Yngwie's cord, pulling it out of the amp on this tour. It was a misstep. Yngwie claimed that Graham had done it on purpose, which was not the case. Yngwie claims to have hit Graham. There was shoving but no hitting. I was standing right there next to them and saw the whole stupid immature episode.

After finishing the Ted Nugent tour, we had three headline shows in California, The De Anza Theater in Riverside, The Fox theater in San Diego, and Perkins Palace in Pasadena. The tension with Yngwie was at its height. We decided to have Steve play the shows on a very short notice to end the chaos. Yngwie was threatening to leave the band, not knowing that he was already replaced by Steve. Fans were shocked to see the new guy in town but none of them left when they heard Steve play. Steve did a great job. We wanted to have made the switch to Steve before the Nugent tour, but Rocshire Records pleaded with us not to make the change until our next album. We agreed, playing all summer across America, knowing that Steve was back in Los Angeles working on new Alcatrazz music for our next album.

We were about to record a new album, Disturbing The Peace, with a terrific new guitarist on a major label. You would think everyone would be happy, but alas, the drama continued.

Toward the end of our summer tour with Ted Nugent, we were offered a chance to switch to Capitol Records. Ray Tuskin, head of A & R, and his assistant, Evie Bozzio, liked the band and wanted to sign us to Capitol. Rocshire had deep pockets but had no idea how to promote a record. They totally blew it with No Parole. We felt Capitol Records would be a better home for us. On August 2nd, 1984, we signed to Capitol Records near the famous intersection of Sunset and Vine. The famous circular tower building that Frank Sinatra and The Beach Boys built welcomed us. We were back in Hollywood. No more driving in bad traffic to Tustin, California in Orange County.

While we were gone, the FBI moved in on Rocky Davis and his Rocshire Record Company. His wife, Shirley, worked for Howard Hughes Medical Group and had embezzled some $24,000,000. She wrote thousands of small checks to Rocky Davis, the religious man who didn't want us drinking cold beer in the 100 plus degree heat. The FBI confiscated everything at Rocshire Records, including personal equipment of the bands that were left behind. We will never know the deals Andy Truman cut with Rocky Davis, but he went from driving an old Cadillac to a newer Rolls Royce. The Feds retrieved $12.000,000 and Rocky and Shirley each got a five-year sentence in a white collar prison. We often wondered when they got out how they spent the missing 12 million.

We rehearsed at Steve's home studio when we returned home and then began recording at Cherokee Studios in Hollywood and Skyline Studios in Topanga Canyon. We hired Eddie Kramer of Jimi Hendrix fame after meeting with him a few months before on tour in New York. We were excited about working together. Eddie has worked with every major rock band of the 60s, 70s, and 80s. Sessions started on September 15th and wrapped up on December 18th, just before Christmas.

In the midst of gearing up for this project, Andy booked a Japanese tour for us. It was not the best decision diplomatically with other Japanese promoters, but it kept the band afloat financially. We left for Tokyo, Osaka, and Nagoya on September 30th, through October 13th. We recorded a live video, and Eddie got to see and hear the band live. We played a few new songs to test them out. Of course, Andy told the video crew to concentrate on Graham and Steve only, leaving the rest of the band out. The guy with everyone's best interest in mind. Steve brought his young guitar tech Ellwood Francis to the band. Ellwood is now the new bass player for ZZ Top.

When we returned to Los Angeles the fires were lit 24/7 to finish by Christmas. Steve was flying in great guitar tracks and Graham worked on the lyrics. With our deadline met, I went to Connecticut for Christmas. Two days later, I drove down to New York City to watch Eddie and George Marino master the new album at Sterling Sound. It was my 33rd birthday.

At the end of February, we teamed up again with Michael Miner to film a video of our son, God Blessed Video. We filmed for two days at S. I. R Sunset, and we used KLOS FM DJ Frazier Smith to play both god and the devil. The video was meant to be amusing rather than trying to be ultra serious. The song would go on to fame on the soundtrack of Grand Theft Auto 1. Vinnie Vincent stopped by to hang out with us and meet Steve Vai. Everything was going in the right direction.

Andy had started a promo war between us and Yngwie, getting us to say bad things about each other. It was wrong because we had no vendetta and wished him well. We were very happy with Steve and the chance to establish ourselves as a musical group of our own style, rather than be a carbon copy of Ritchie Blackmore's world. I'm very proud of Disturbing The Peace. We entered a new musical territory of creativity that I felt set us apart from many other bands. One of my favorite tracks is Desert Diamond, a low heavy song about the Pyramids in the dropped key of C. In the song Mercy, I was tasked on a Sunday to go out and find an English to Hindu translation of the lyric "brother son and sister moon" for the second verse. Graham sang the lyric phonetically from what Indian shopkeepers explained to me. The song was about the killing of the Bengal tigers from the tigers' point of view. Will You Be Home Tonight was about James Dean dying. The bass pulsates relentlessly through the song, emulating a heartbeat. We came up another level as a band, and I wish we could have done another album with Steve.

In June we split with Andy. we lost out on a co-headline a twenty city American tour with Uli Roth. He had abandoned us at Capitol, sinking our new album and devoting all his time to Yngwie, who didn't ask any questions about his business matters. Andy took full advantage of that. I told Andy more than once that he should manage the two new guitar heroes together under one roof, but he wouldn't listen. Yngwie couldn't be God if Steve was also. It turned out that a few years later, Steve and Joe Satrianni became very successful and helped Yngwie's career by adding him to their G3 guitar tours.

Chapter 19

A tour of six shows was undertaken with the Canadian band Helix in Texas. We were Capitol Records label mates. Being from the Great White North, they didn't add air conditioning to their tour bus. They really regretted that in the heat of a Texas summer. Great guys to tour with. With two albums under our belts, we had a more interesting set list that was fun to play. At this point, Steve was offered a deal he couldn't refuse– just like KISS had offered Vinnie Vincent. David Lee Roth was starting his own band and out of all the guitarists in the world he could replace Eddie Van Halen with, he chose Steve. It was a setback for us. We wished Steve well and we are good friends today. We certainly didn't see that coming. Another unexpected moment in the best made plans of mice and men.

Myself, and Jimmy Waldo took a meeting with Tim Collins, about managing Alcatrazz. He had just resurrected Aerosmith and got them a multi-million dollar deal with Sony Records. It felt good with our Boston roots connection, but we all felt that with us being based in L.A. and Tim in Boston that it would be a problem for communication on a day-to-day basis. We had the good fortune to sign with Wendy Dio instead, of Niji Management in Los Angeles. Wendy was Ronnie Dio's wife and manager. With the addition of Alcatrazz, she had two great Rainbow singers under one roof. It felt right and Wendy had a sound reputation in the music business. The search was on for a third guitarist. Carmine Appice's brother, Vinnie, played drums for Ronnie Dio. He had worked with guitarist Danny Johnson and suggested we contact him. Danny had played with Rick Derringer, Rod Stewart, and Alice Cooper. A phone call to his home in Shreveport, Louisiana was made and Danny agreed to come out to Los Angeles to audition for us. We were in strange times musically in the late 80's, and thought maybe we would tone the guitar virtuoso aspect down a notch. In hindsight, we should have stayed the course. You're driving down the road at high speed and things are jumping out at you; you can't avoid everything.

Andy had torpedoed our Disturbing The Peace album, and now it was Graham's turn to finish things off. In early summer of 1986, we settled into American Recording Studios to record our third studio album, Dangerous Games, with Richie Podolor as producer. Richie's career went back to recording Sandy Nelson's Let There Be Drums, Steppenwolf, and Three Dog Night. He was also an accomplished session guitarist. We recorded there until June 23rd, after a tumultuous six months of changing direction and songwriting. We'd spent two months rehearsing new material with sketchy names of song titles.

It wasn't fair to lay blame on Danny Johnson alone for the record having been different from our others. Danny was an excellent guitar player, but he was not acquainted with the more European guitar shredding style the band was known for. Steve Vai had graciously spent time with him, showing him how the previous songs should be played. The new material was not in the same vein as we had done before. We had to make adjustments in our style.

I've worked with Jimmy Waldo in five bands, and I have high praise for the General Contractor Of Rock. He can do everything from creating extremely creative keyboard parts to constructing innovative musical hardware. Jimmy does it all, and without complaint. He and Danny spent time trying to piece things together. It wasn't so much that there was a toss-up over heavier vs pop, so much as it was the lyrics Graham continued writing. The only big success Graham has ever known was written by outside writer, Russ Ballard. Roger Glover of Rainbow had insisted Graham sing more rock and roll lyrics, which Graham scoffed at but consented. Lyrics about the Blue Boar and Ohayo Tokyo were clever innuendos that no one understood and no one bought. He insisted on rerecording a song that he had recorded on a previous album from the 60s called Only One Woman. It was a waltz in 3/4 time that was much more suited to Dancing With The Stars than on an Alcatrazz record. Another cover was It's My Life by The Animals. I envisioned it as a heavy anthem of independence, but it came out sounding toothless.

Capitol Records became very worried about the situation. The big guns from A&R came to the studio to try and make sense of things and offer their experience. Ray Tuskin and Don Greerson were coming off a massive hit by our Capitol Records label mates, Heart. Their record sold six million copies and they were touring the world from it for a third time. Heart had worked with Ray and Don and used outside writers for their album and never looked back. We were offered songs by Bryan Adams and my friend Holly Knight. This has been the role of Artist and Repertoire departments since records were invented but to no avail.

Graham would not see the light and thought he would make more money through publishing if he was part of the song writing. That's true if you sell a lot of records. He just didn't get it or understand the politics of teamwork. It's one thing to question a record company, but Graham alienated everyone. That made Richie Podolor crazy, as he had produced all of the Three Dog Night albums. They were one of the biggest bands in the 70's and they did nothing but sing cover songs written by other people. They had 21 Top 40 hits and are still performing.

The other faction that set this album apart from our previous albums was a total lack of guitar and guitar solos. It was all minimalized. The record was recorded very well by Richie, but he was adamant about not featuring the guitar. Wendy Dio bless her heart, championed for more heavy guitar, but to no avail. Danny described it as, "That dog don't hunt."

Dangerous Games, written by Danny, should have been a big hit song, but it, too, came out too light and homogenized for our fans. We lost our core fanbase and didn't make any new ones for our transgressions. There are many who like Dangerous Games, but unfortunately for us, not enough. The album was released on August 21st, 1986. In October we toured the Midwest with Jefferson Starship. They didn't appreciate our humor of us playing their song Jane at soundchecks. In Ann Arbor, Michigan, Grace Slick held my 6 month old daughter, Tyler, in her arms backstage. That was quite something after seeing Grace at Woodstock with the sun coming up singing Volunteers of America. She was very, very cool.

We did a twenty five city tour with the band Rough Cutt, also managed by Wendy, which was uncomfortable having to share a bus together. Nice guys, but no breathing room. On New Year's Eve we played a concert at the Santa Monica Civic Center with the Christian band Stryper. Their audience were throwing quarters at us screaming we were the Devil and sang satanic songs. I made an extra $10 that night in change.

In January, with the New Year coming in, artistic differences brought down the house. Because of Graham's aversion to playing ball with Ray Tuskin and Don Greerson, Capitol Records was dropping the band from their roster. No fourth album. Wendy Dio also let the band go from Niji Management.

I had just turned 35 a few days before and had a 9-month-old daughter. It was time to make some adjustments in my life.

Chapter 20

And so, it was every man for himself once again. There should be music courses on how to swim from sinking ships. Collision shops for damaged bands. Graham went to live with his wife's family in Adelaide, Australia, going as far off the radar as possible for a few years. Jimmy began a string of recording projects as an in-demand session keyboard player and producer. Jan had a few more drum gigs before retiring to New Hampshire. Danny managed to have a very good 15-year run as lead guitarist for Steppenwolf. It's funny how the band Steppenwolf keeps appearing. New England did a one-off show with Steppenwolf and Uriah Heep at a rodeo fairground in Beaumont, Texas in 1981.

My friend Scott Sheets, ex guitarist of the Pat Benatar Band, hired me for a project he was producing. Manako and The Wildcats were a very popular all female band in Japan. Their record label felt they weren't up to recording the record and called Scott to put a recording band together to play on the album in Los Angeles. Ace session guitarist Tim Pierce came in. Myron Grombacher from Pat Benatar's band and Frank Briggs from the funk group Atlantic Starr played drums. Mark Stein, keyboard player for The Vanilla Fudge, joined Rudy Sarzo from Quiet Riot and myself on bass. It was fun to record and everyone was paid well. We did a song called Loving You With My Eyes that Scott had written with Jonathan Cain from Journey. We also did a cool version of Helter Skelter. This is the kind of situation where you have to be there to participate in. It was the reason I was living in Los Angeles. In today's world with computer programs like Pro Tools, it's now possible to live in separate countries and record albums– as we do now in the modern lineup of Alcatrazz. Back then it was imperative to be where the action was.

A disc jockey friend of mine from the metal radio station KMET Fm called one night. He wanted to know if I would like to fill in on bass with a new country band called Marshall Lewis and The Law. The band was very good. The Palomino club is the closest venue on the West Coast to The Grand Ole Opry in Nashville. All of the most famous country stars have played there over the years. I had driven by it hundreds of times on Lankershim Blvd., right near MCA and Davlen Studios, always thinking that was one gig I'd never play. I brought in my good friend Scott Rath on pedal steel guitar to the band and we played The Palomino twice. I've known Scott for years from back in my Boston days when he played in the band Zachariah. He's a great guitarist and really makes the steel guitar sing. We played one night at Sasch in Studio City, and the great Buddy Miles came up and played drums with us. Unfortunately, our leader, Jimmy Lewis, developed personal problems and the band folded midway through recording an album.

I had a very good friend named Layne Bednar who was an excellent bass player. He was a good-looking guy with blonde hair. He told me he could pass auditions musically but being 6 feet 5 he was too tall for most bands to hire. At 6 feet tall myself I know the feeling of towering over everyone in a band photo. "Imagine" I said, "if you could find a talented group of guys who are all 6 foot 5 or taller." "Then" I added, "we could call the band GOLIATH, The Biggest Band In The World!" We decided to go for it, and with my help we found four other heavy metal rock players in the L.A. area all over 6 foot 5. It was impressive seeing these guys standing together, and they were very good musically.

I couldn't believe running into Andy Truman one day in Laurel Canyon traffic. There he was, driving a brand new BMW convertible. We pulled over and started talking. I told him about GOLIATH and he got excited, wanting to help manage the band. I sensed danger, but I thought maybe he had changed his ways and he could help the guys. He came over to my place a week later with a contract proposal that gave us each $20,000.00 and the band got peanuts. I contend that people don't change, they just get older. It was tempting, looking at my three kids all under the age of six. I said no way, I'm not doing that. Andy left, never to be seen again, and GOLIATH became another L.A. band that never got off the ground.

Jonas Hanson was the lead Guitarist of the Swedish band Silver Mountain. Some of its members moved to Los Angeles to play on Yngwie's first album, and Jonas followed. We were introduced to each other through a friend and hit it off very well. He's a great guy and a terrific guitarist. Soon we were playing together, and we added Jan Uvena on drums. Jonas was working as a recording engineer, which allowed us free studio time to make a CD together. Mike Stone was a guitarist in the band Queensryche and contributed lead vocals. We made a video—which Jonas is very good at—and began mixing the recording.

Then we were all jolted out of our beds one morning at 4 am. The Northridge Earthquake destroyed the San Fernando Valley, killing 56 people in our area. There was chaos and over 2000 aftershocks. In the ensuing days we slept outside in our car with the three kids in the back seat as the house wasn't safe. Los Angeles is a city built on the dry desert. It relies on the water from the Colorado River miles away. If anything ever cut that off, it would be sheer anarchy in the streets– not a good place to be if that happens. I was ready to make a change at this point in my life. I was ready for the bridge. "Take me to the bridge" as James Brown sang.

Every truck was rented at this time, and it's estimated that one million people left Los Angeles County after the quake. Somehow my wife found a moving company that would take us away from the mayhem and the cutthroat music business. We decided to move to Lake St. Clair in Michigan, where we could raise our family in a more stable and normal environment, rather than in the land of Valley Girls.

The Jonas Hansson Band CD, titled One, was released a few months later, and I am very pleased with that record. If the timing had been better, Jonas would have been the perfect replacement for Steve Vai in Alcatrazz. Add earthquakes to the list of things that can come out of nowhere and royally change your routine.

I stood along the shoreline in deep snow, gazing up at the twinkling stars on a freezing cold and cloudless evening. It reminded me of Doctor Zhivago, exiled to the deep winter of Siberia. I watched as the moon cast its light along the frozen Lake St. Clair. The air was clean, and no smog could be seen. There was a feeling of serenity knowing that my three children could walk to elementary, middle, and high school from our new home across the street.

We had played Detroit many times with both New England and Alcatrazz. New England played the Pontiac Silverdome with KISS. Alcatrazz played Cobo Hall once with Eddie Money, and another time with Ted Nugent. Both bands had headlined Harpo's Concert Theater many times. We always had a great time there, but never in my wildest dreams did I ever think I would move there.

It was now the 21st Century. The Motown scene was on a much smaller scale than what I'd been used to. There were no major record companies there, or bands playing the style of rock that I was looking for. I'm very grateful, though, to have played with some great guitarists and drummers in Detroit over the years.

Erich Goebel, the Blues King of Clubs, melts the town down on a nightly basis, and is always so kind to let me sit in. My friend Paul Kramer of FJT and The Igniters and I recorded two CD's, along with drum virtuoso Pat DeLeon of Imminent Sonic Destruction, plus our friend Steve black, DJ supreme at WRIF FM on vocals. Paul was also a product manager at Korg/Vox. I helped design patches for the Korg Pandora 1, 2, and Pandora 1000 multi-effect processors along with friend and bassist Stu Hamm. Jamie Wagner, Mark Chuddy, and I had a band called Second Hand Smoke. We had a ton of great times burning up the bar scene with some classic guitar oriented rock.

Some of the best live gigs I played at the time were playing acoustically with my friend Chris Degnore, a fine singer and guitarist. Just my acoustic electric bass and his acoustic guitar, playing songs by The Faces and other favorites of ours. We had a lot of fun. Last but not least, is my dear friend Leonard Johnson, drummer and artist, the Mayor of the Cass Corridor. Leonard, who hosts jams in his Royal Oak basement nightclub, airbrushed Salvador Dali's The Persistence Of Memory on my Wishnevsky acoustic bass. It's a masterpiece. I have some great memories of the Motor City.

In 2004, Jimmy called me to say that John's wife, Gail, had suddenly passed and was leaving him with two kids in high school. Gail had been a good friend of the band, and we are sorry for her loss. Jimmy, Hirsh, and I decided to give John a visit in Boston to cheer him up. Our reunion was remarkable, and we had a great time reminiscing and laughing. We also recorded two new songs while we were there which we were really pleased with.

Hirsh went a step further and suggested we play the next year at the Benefit For Women's Social Services, put on by Steven Tyler of Aerosmith and other Boston luminaries. At first we said no way, but we warmed up to the idea and made plans to play at the concert on May 12th, 2005.

We played in Medford, Massachusetts at the Chevalier Theater with The James Montgomery Band, Charlie Farren of the Joe Perry Project, and others. We had not played together in 23 years. We didn't know what to expect, but when the curtain went up it was like we never left. I had that thrilling rocket launch feeling and halfway through the first song I looked around and said we got this! Three of our songs were selected for the live CD that was recorded, called Music For Middlesex.

Our reunion went so smoothly that we decided to play at the next benefit. A year later I called my friend Dale Bozzio, who is a Bostonian, to see if she and her band would like to be on the show and she agreed. Missing Persons was added as the headliner. The show went well for us, but after our set there was a huge summer lightning storm that knocked out the power of the theater for over an hour. Unfortunately for Dale, the audience had dwindled from 1000 people to about 200.

Over the years we have done a trio of concerts three times. We play at The Spire Theater in Plymouth, Mass. The Bull Run in Andover, Mass., and Grand Oaks Live in Los Angeles. We have an amazing group of fans who have come to see us from the four corners of the country, as well as England and Japan.

In 2013 we played another show in Boston at The Cafe Royale for The Channel Reunion Concert. The Channel was a large club on the waterfront in the 80s, and both New England and Alcatrazz had played there. This was our third charity event and we played with a half dozen local Boston artists. We had a great time and stole the show. It was very rewarding because our kids got to see New England for the first time.

The next year, in 2014, we did our own concert at The Regent Theater in Arlington Massachusetts. It was a great venue and we recorded our Live at The Regent Theater CD there. The following day we did a show at Thrifties in Manchester, New Hampshire. A year later we released our new single I Know There's Something Here, which got very good reviews. In 2018 New England played in Tokyo, Japan. It was four months before Jimmy and I would play there again as Alcatrazz. I have played in Japan with Alcatrazz three times, but it was really rewarding to play there with New England. Our last trio of shows was in 2019, just before Covid moved in. I know to never say never, and I hope that more music from New England comes along.

Through the miracle of the internet I was also able to reconnect with my friend, David Cooper, in London. We were able to record with our friends, Herman Rarebell in Germany and Peter French, also in London, with Protools. We stitched together some of our old songs under the name of the Cooper Shea Band. It was great to hear the music again from my time in London in the early 70's. I always wondered what might have happened to the band if Herman and I didn't have to leave over work permit issues. Everyone played well and we self-released the ten songs on YouTube and Spotify. It was wonderful getting a chance to redo our unfinished music that we were prevented from doing so long ago in the early 70's. I was so glad to be in contact again with a great group of guys, continuing our music decades later and thousands of miles apart.

There was a great sense of momentum building up. New England being back on the map was somewhat surreal to me. My wish of reuniting had come true. I felt like I was riding a 21st Century asteroid across the sky, as two more musical situations were rising up in Los Angeles. Both opportunities would keep me very busy musically, and well traveled.

As New England continued to play live, Jimmy Waldo asked me if I would like to be part of a new recording project he was part of in 2016. It included his friends Tommy Fields, a very successful film composer, guitarist, and singer in Los Angeles, and D.

Kendall Jones, an ace session guitarist from Shreveport, Louisiana with orchestral arranging degrees from Berklee College in Boston and UCLA. The music was very heavy and modern, incorporating many influences, one of which was Alcatrazz. The recording was done around and in between everyone's schedules. Spencer Spectrum stepped in to play drums. We did a version of the Alcatrazz song, Hiroshima. Jimmy wrote a beautiful piece of dreamy music for the ending, complementing this song's original lyrics. As a homage to Alcatrazz, I came up with the name Rock Island Orchestra. In 2019 a digital CD was released under the title Revolution on Cherry Red Records. It can be heard on YouTube and all other digital platforms. We have talked about doing another record if we all can find the time.

At the end of 2016 Graham Bonnet's manager, Giles Lavery, had called with an interesting proposal. Giles is a brilliant strategist and a no-nonsense kind of guy. Jimmy had recorded with the Graham Bonnet band and had recently joined on for touring as well. An idea was put forth of possibly having me come on the road and do an Alcatrazz set after the Graham Bonnet Band was finished. Graham, Jimmy, and I would use Graham's guitarist and drummer and play a set of Alcatrazz songs. They asked if I was interested and I said yes, definitely.

In January I left for Los Angeles to begin rehearsing for three shows in Texas and a follow-up show in Reno, Nevada. It was fun to play the Alcatrazz songs again with Graham and Jimmy. The Texas dates went really well. In March we were booked in Japan for three concerts in Osaka, Nagoya, and Tokyo. The shows were a great success and a live DVD was recorded and released on Frontier Records. Later in the year, in October 2018 Jimmy and I were brought together again playing New England shows in Boston and Los Angeles.

I was invited to play at the KISS convention in Helsinki, Finland in November when I got home. I was asked to attend by super host Marko Syrjala through my connection to the KISS family. I'm actually on their family tree twice: Once as a member of New England and another for being a member of Warrior with Vinnie Vincent. I played live with ex KISS guitarist Bruce Kulick, and with Bobby Rock on drums. We played one of Vinnie Vincent's songs, Lick It Up. Strange, but not as strange as eating asphalt flavored ice cream that the Finnish people love as a treat. I spent two days giving interviews, signing autographs, and doing a little sightseeing. I had a lot of fun and was treated very well by Marko and his network of friends.

Chapter 21

When I got back home to the U.S., Giles called and asked if I would join Alcatrazz full-time. The Graham Bonnet Band could only go so far. If we had three original members of Alcatrazz, we could get a record deal and really tear it up. Joe Stump, shred master and associate professor of music at Berklee College of Music, had recently joined the band and he would come over to Alcatrazz, as well as the hard-hitting Latin Lion, drummer Mark Banquechea. I said yes. In 2019 we signed a five record deal with Silver Lining Records in England.

With all systems go, we proceeded to record the fourth Alcatrazz studio album, titled Born Innocent. We wanted a celebration of our music and had many guests recording with us like Bob Kulick, Chris Impelliterri, and D. Kendall Jones. Steve Vai contributed the track Dirty Like The City. On March 27th 2020, at the beginning of the Covid pandemic, Jimmy, Joe and I flew to Los Angeles to shoot a group photo with Graham and Mark. It was scary being in a large plane with less than 30 passengers. The album Born Innocent was released later that summer on August 7th, 2020, reaching #1 in Burn magazine in Japan. We were all very proud of that.

Out of nowhere Graham Bonnet quit Alcatrazz, leaving us in a quandary, regardless of his being signed to a record contract. He said he didn`t want to sing heavy metal. Giles immediately called Doogie White in Edinburgh, Scotland on behalf of Alcatrazz. Doogie, like Graham, had also played and recorded with Ritchie Blackmore, Michael Schenker, and Yngwie Malmsteen. It was a perfect fit for both Alcatrazz and Doogie. He said yes to joining Alcatrazz and we all moved on with a strong lineup and determination to press on.

The Covid situation destroyed our plans for an extensive European tour with our friends from Girlschool at the time. Everything was canceled with no plans to play live. It was decided we would begin work on a new album with Doogie singing. The album was our fifth Alcatrazz studio album with the Roman numeral V, or 'V' for Victory as a title. We got great reviews and charged forward. With Covid winding down, we embarked on a U.K. Tour of twelve shows in England, Scotland, and Wales. We had rehearsed for a week at Panic Rehearsal Studio, beginning November 1st in London. This was our first time playing live with Dougie at the helm. Mark Banquechea had decided to stay in Los Angeles, and Larry Paterson from the Blaze Bayley Band was brought in on drums. As well as being an excellent drummer, he is an international authority on German U boats, having written over twenty books on the subject. Our first show at the Hard Rock Nights Festival in Yarmouth went extremely well. Back at our hotel that night we recorded the theme song for 'Joe's Deli,' to much hollering and laughter in the kitchen. Joe knows all the hard guitar notes as well as where to find the best IPA beer and snacks all over the world. I got to see my good friends Michael Corby in Scotland and David Cooper in London and talk about old times. The tour was terrific and after four weeks, Joe, Jimmy and I got back to the States, getting around the Covid confusion happening at Heathrow airport.

After the Holidays we began recording our sixth studio album, Take No Prisoners, with remote recordings from Boston, Scotland, Italy, Chicago, and Florida. Our lovely lady friends from Girlschool sang background vocals on the track Don't Get Mad Get Even. The band now had three albums from the 80's, and three in the 21st century. Our

Born Innocent album sold so well that Silver Lining Records released a double LP record on blue vinyl.

The music business has a mantra: tour record, tour record, tour record, repeat. It's a rigorous schedule where you have a short time to create magic in a recording studio. Then you are subjected to a grueling live tour that can mean a different hotel in a different state or country daily, taxing your health and humor. When I was a teenager I marveled at the adventure of it. As an adult I am adjusted to the reality of life on the road, and I am very grateful for the opportunity to keep rockin' around the world.

After the completion of our new CD, Take No Prisoners, we met in Essen Germany. A week of rehearsals began before starting our 2022 Summer Tour of Europe. The weather was warm and sunny with no rain during the month that we were gone. We chose Essen because of its proximity to our first show in Liege, Belgium. Our tour was sixteen shows in nine countries, all done in less than three weeks. We played Belgium, Italy, Germany, Netherlands, France, Spain, Portugal, and Switzerland with our final gig in Austria. Again, we played with our good friends from Girlschool. The shows were sweltering hot and the crowds were super. Jimmy and I share stage right together. Every once in a while on stage we grin like Cheshire cats knowing that here we are, rocking in our 70's, having as much fun as when we first met in our 20's.

As the future unveils itself, I look forward to playing bass, or my collection of various sized ukuleles, for just as long as I can. The music business can be brutal, but that one hour on stage playing to our fans is well worth the long travel times and hardship and sacrifice. There is nothing like it. Nothing can take the place of playing live and making people happy. I'm very lucky to have been able to follow this road for six decades, navigating the minefields, meeting hundreds of amazing friends, and visiting so many wonderful places. What sets the music business apart from others is its tremendous lack of security. It throws every pitfall it can at you, trying to wear down your endurance and creative willpower. If you pass the testing, It can be yours though drive, determination, and a dash of luck. I have nothing but the deepest respect for all musicians in all genres at all levels who devote themselves to music and entertaining others. Best wishes to all and keep rockin'.

Never take no for an answer.

Chapter 22
Conclusion

Over 60 years have gone by since I first started playing music. Rather than write a tell-all book of rock and roll parties and mischief, I wanted to write a story about development and continuity. How does a teenager with no childhood musical instruction walk into a store, buy an instrument, achieve gold and platinum records, and play on some of the world's most iconic stages? My background sketches hopefully answer some of these questions.

I've always wondered if I followed the bass or did it follow me? It's been a tremendous friend through good times and bad. It challenges me on a daily basis to better myself and explore the world in awe. I hope my story is an inspiration to young musicians everywhere who share the dream of a musical journey. With great determination, goals are achievable. A huge, heartfelt thank you to my family and my friends for helping make mine come true.

Always remember, No Bass No Party!

www.ingramcontent.com/pod-product-compliance
Lightning Source LLC
Chambersburg PA
CBHW061756290426
44109CB00030B/2873